Dear Patricia

Blessings on your wealth? well-being 🖤

Love,
Keven

The
MONEY
Keys

LIFESUCCESS PUBLISHING, LLC
8900 E Pinnacle Peak Road, Suite D240
Scottsdale, AZ 85255

Telephone:	800.473.7134
Fax:	480.661.1014
E-mail:	admin@lifesuccesspublishing.com
ISBN:	978-1-59930-050-4
Cover :	Patti Knoles & LifeSuccess Publishing
Layout:	Lloyd Arbour & LifeSuccess Publishing

COMPANIES, ORGANIZATIONS, INSTITUTIONS, AND INDUSTRY PUB-LICATIONS: Quantity discounts are available on bulk purchases of this book for reselling, educational purposes, subscription incentives, gifts, sponsorship, or fundraising. Special books or book excerpts can also be created to fit specific needs such as private labeling with your logo on the cover and a message from a VIP printed inside. For more information please contact our Special Sales Department at LifeSuccess Publishing.

Printed in Canada

The
MONEY
Keys

Unlocking Peace,
Freedom & Real Financial Power

KAREN RUSSO

Praise for Karen Russo's
The Money Keys

"The beautiful being I know as Rev. Karen Russo is a faithful servant, student and teacher of universal spiritual principles."

- Michael Bernard Beckwith,
founder Agape International Spiritual Center and featured in *The Secret* movie

"Karen Russo is a powerful and intelligent teacher who weaves together an unusual blend of business education with timeless spiritual truths. You are richly blessed to be encountering this important material."

- Bob Proctor,
featured in *The Secret* movie and author of *You Were Born Rich*

"Realizing your vision and identifying your values are keys to everything you do in life and in wealth building. Karen Russo understands this. She helps you apply spiritual principles and tools which keep you on your fastest path to cash. Karen's the real deal and can get you real results!"

- Loral Langemeier,
founder & CEO of Live Out Loud and author of the national bestseller
The Millionaire Maker

"Mastering the inner game of wealth requires conscious commitment to continuously expanding what you believe, what you say and what you do. Karen Russo does a great job of showing you how spiritual principles apply to our everyday money lives. Don't just read *The Money Keys*; use the tools to grow yourself while you grow your wealth."

- **T. Harv Eker,**
Author #1 Bestseller, New York Times, USA Today, Wall Street Journal,
Secrets of the Millionaire Mind™

"An important new teacher is here! Karen Russo is smart, clear and entertaining as she shares a fresh perspective on money matters. Use these tools to conceive, create and enjoy your vision of a wealthy life."

- **Vic Johnson,**
founder of AsAManThinketh.net and author of *Day by Day with James Allen*

"Successful achievers embody the power of the human spirit. In *The Money Keys*, Karen Russo shares inspiring stories of people who exhibited an indefatigable spirit to create financial success and shows you how you can, too."

- **Cynthia Kersey, best-selling author of** *Unstoppable* **and** *Unstoppable Women*

"Karen Russo is a sister teacher in breaking through the trance of scarcity. She helps us feel, see and know that our spiritual connection is essential for discovering true peace about money, about supply and about our lives."

- **Victoria Castle, author of** *The Trance of Scarcity*

"Karen Russo is a radiant and powerful woman as well as a deeply insightful and gifted spiritual teacher. Prepare to be celebrated and unleashed in ways you've not even dared to dream possible."

- Katherine Woodward Thomas,
MFT, author of *Calling in "The One": 7 Weeks to Attracting the Love of Your Life*

"Women who lead rich lives develop financial savvy, adopt positive behaviors and strategies, and engage in continual self-improvement. Karen Russo provides powerful ideas for integrating spirituality and money to keep you motivated and moving forward."

- Lois P. Frankel, PhD,
author of *Nice Girls Don't Get Rich* **and** *See Jane Lead*

"If you want to finally find the success you've been seeking, you must be able to quickly identify and unlock the emotional barriers to success. Karen Russo shows you how to practically apply universal principles to instantly win the inner success game. Get this book NOW!"

- Stephanie Frank,
best-selling author of *The Accidental Millionaire*

"Karen Russo wants you to know and to feel your connection to the spiritual realities of abundance, peace, freedom and expansion. The practical tools in *The Money Keys* will help you to give your gifts to life and receive the bounty of the invisible and visible supply that is your birthright."

- Diane Harmony,
author of award-winning *5 GIFTS for an*
Abundant Life: Create a Consciousness of Wealth

"Truly prosperous people train themselves to choose their thoughts carefully to be in line with the Universal Laws that Karen Russo beautifully describes in *The Money Keys*. If you want to strengthen your capacity to co-create true wealth in your life, this book is for you."

- **Leslie Householder,**
author, *The Jackrabbit Factor: Why You Can* **and** *Hidden Treasures: Heaven's Astonishing Help with Your Money Matters*

"Life is good because the Spirit does not contradict its own nature of goodness. The spiritual laws that govern our universe exist for our use in co-creating the Spirit's vision for our life and life on our planet."

– Michael Bernard Beckwith

Dedication

*I dedicate everything to my beloved hero Bill.
Sharing my life with you is the greatest investment
I'll ever make. Every tangible and intangible asset
and even the seeming liabilities have returned
unlimited love, growth, joy and freedom! You have
provided me a life beyond my wildest dreams.
Indeed, we are already wealthy.*

Acknowledgments

I am deeply grateful to my wonderful parents, Joe and Nancy Russo, for their constant support, encouragement and generosity.

I've been blessed with magnificent brothers, Tony and Bill. We also share our lives with an extended family that includes Beth, Bel and Bea, as well as Billy, Michael, Jessica and Mason, and all the Russos and Sneeds. Thank you for the gifts that you are.

My spiritual family is a great source of inspiration for me. You have introduced me to the peace that passes human understanding, the freedom to co-create life with a loving universe, and the joy of sharing the journey! To my prayer partners Jennifer, Nancy, Mark Anthony, Janice, Paul, Liz and Brita, I am blessed by your spiritual strength. In our vision group, including Cynthia, Denise and Wanice, we have shared loving inspiration for years. The beauty mastery girls, including Jenny B, Amy, Ginny, Deborah, Kate and Marilyn, have been a breath of fresh air and radiance in my life. I celebrate each one of you.

I've been uplifted by many spiritual teachers, programs and prophecies, both ancient and contemporary. The New Thought/ Ancient Wisdom teachings have opened the doorway to the limitless power of God that is not dependent upon circumstance or opinion. Thank you to Ernest Holmes, Bill Wilson and Dr. Bob, to Dr. Michael Beckwith, Rev. Nirvana Gayle, Rev. Diane Harmony, Katherine Woodward Thomas and more. I offer special appreciation to the spiritual communities of Agape, Namaste and New Vision.

To my mastermind partners in wealth-building, I thank you. The practical strategies of Loral Langemeier and Live Out Loud opened up the business possibilities that allowed the vision of this book to come into reality.

To every client, student and reader who contributed ideas and feedback for the content, tools and practices of *The Money Keys*, thank you. I especially thank Suzanne M, Kim, Heather and all who were willing to have their stories shared. This book is for you and by you.

To all who have contributed creativity and hard work in getting these ideas from the invisible into the visible, including Gerry, Bob, Patti, Dee, Paula, Ruby, Kathleen, the brilliant and committed Kandi Miller and the whole team at LifeSuccess Publishing, thank you.

We all owe a special acknowledgment to our dear Suzanne E. In addition to everything she does for us, she prays to celebrate the abundance of spirit revealing powerfully in me and in each one of you, our readers.

Author's Note

The stories and personal examples in this book reflect facts, feelings and experiences that many readers can relate to. While the essential ideas of the stories are all real, some represent composites of individual interviews and personal observations. Names and other characteristics have been changed to respect privacy.

Foreword

You *were* born rich! That title rings with truth on so many levels, but to really live and experience that which is your birthright, you must develop a prosperity consciousness. This is done, not through memorization but through a deep understanding and application of universal principles.

This important book, *The Money Keys*, offers vital information to help you expand into real financial power and mastery. Karen Russo is a powerful and intelligent teacher who weaves together an unusual blend of business education with timeless spiritual truths. She assists entrepreneurs, and business professionals to strengthen their understanding of spiritual principles and shares specific tactics for applying universal law to attain desired goals, regardless of past or present circumstances.

Have you ever wondered why the rich get richer and the poor get poorer? It's not just an old wives' tale, for the most part, it's a fact. Money is an idea, a concept. There's nothing magical about getting rich; it's a science. The only real requisite to earning a lot of money, to a life that offers financial freedom is the decision to do so.

When most people think about money, they relate it to lack and limitation, because of their conditioning or paradigm. They are their own prisoner, but they're not aware of that so it never occurs to them they can set themselves free, that they have the ability to change anything they want in their life ... all it takes is a decision.

If we think back to all of the things we heard about money when we were growing up, it's no wonder people have the hang-ups they do concerning money. Do any of these statements sound familiar to you? Money doesn't grow on ____. Money won't make you ____. Or, money is the root of all ____. I know for certainty you were able to repeat the last word of each of those statements from memory. It would almost appear that we were raised by the same parents!

In the blockbuster hit, *The Secret*, in which I was very fortunate to take part, it clearly explains that like attracts like, or we attract that which we are in harmony with. For centuries, all of the great teachers have agreed on this one point, yet very few people understand this truth.

I believe the world is experiencing a spiritual awakening that is unprecedented. Millions of people are becoming aware of the truth that our well-being isn't dependent upon anything outside of us; everything we need is inside. We've been taught to live through our physical senses ... we can hear, see, smell, taste and touch. Well, so can animals! Why didn't anyone ever teach us that we were also gifted with a phenomenal set of mental faculties ... intuition, memory, the will, reason, and imagination. It's these faculties that allow us to live from the inside out. It takes the same amount of energy to live a life of lack and limitation as it does to live one of prosperity and abundance. Why not choose what you want! It only takes a decision to get out of survival mode into a life of magnificent abundance!

The late Eric Hoffer stated, "To learn you need a certain degree of confidence, not too much and not too little. If you have too little confidence you'll think you cannot learn and if you have too much, you'll think you don't have to learn." I tend to agree with him.

In this book, Karen shares how you can find your way on your own Money Map toward a vision that is spiritually uplifting with a belief system that is mentally empowering and emotionally involving, and practical habits that help you to be the best you can be.

Spirit is always for expansion and fuller expression. Enjoy the full manifestation of the greatness that is within you.

– **Bob Proctor**
Featured in *The Secret* **movie**
Author of *You Were Born Rich*

Table of Contents

Introduction

Money and Our Quest for Spiritual Fulfillment

"Prosperity is a way of living and thinking, and not just money or things. Poverty is a way of living and thinking, and not just a lack of money or things."

– Eric Butterworth

The Beginning

"You must be a good girl and behave nicely to build up grace for yourself in this life," Sister Elizabeth said. "We obey God's rules here so that we can go to heaven when we die."

I was eleven years old, and I respected Sister because she was my teacher. I felt the grace that she was talking about. It filled my heart with a sweet sense of peace. But I also remember questioning her words. How could this peaceful feeling inside of me be something that I had to earn?

The grace plan that Sister described sounded like a savings plan. I had my navy blue bank book, in which the deposits of allowance, gifts from relatives and earnings from baby-sitting were tracked in my savings account. But the idea of applying this method to grace didn't feel right. "Aren't we already full of grace? Don't we come here that way? Why do we have to save up grace in the 'grace bank' for a later time?"

Something within me knew that in the midst of the traditional religious teachings were spiritual truths of freedom and possibility here and now, not just after death. I felt a sense, even as a child, that human beings are made in the image and likeness of a larger reality, and that our nature, being one with the universal nature, must be complete, infinite and whole already. I knew that we don't need to earn grace; we *are* grace!

At only eleven years old, I was not quite so lofty in my language and philosophy. But I sure didn't like starting from nothing and having to earn grace. It was a moment of divine discontent and the beginning of a contemplation of ideas that would emerge as this book decades later.

My Own Path

Today I'm still interested in grace, banking, spiritual philosophy and how it all fits with money. With an MBA from Columbia University, I've enjoyed years of accomplishment in corporate businesses and have created an interesting and diverse portfolio of real estate and financial investments. I'm also an ordained minister in Religious Science, a teaching that synthesizes religious ideas, philosophical truths and scientific principles about how life works. My life is dedicated to practicing and sharing how universal spiritual principles express themselves in our everyday lives.

When it comes to our money, I firmly believe that cultivating our spirituality, beliefs and habits around money is as important as developing our capacity to earn, invest, exchange, grow and understand it. With my background, I'm destined to speak, teach and write about the interconnectedness of money and its meaning in our lives.

I grew up in a family in which personal intimacy and our relationship to the world at large was expressed through education, work and money. Some families show love through food and cooking, sharing the family business or playing sports or hobbies together. We express our love, respect and interest in each other through noticing and appreciating what we know, what we teach and what we do. Many of those intangible concepts are "tracked" through earning, spending and saving money.

My father grew up on the East Coast as the son of Italian immigrants. He finished high school with a net worth of $500, which he invested in his own education. He was one of the first in his family to go to college and worked his way through school by taking jobs in railroad construction and translating for the Spanish-speaking workers at a food factory. After completing his education, my father worked in various jobs for the United States government as an economist.

My father earned a middle-class income, but he systematically saved ten percent of that income, used "dollar cost averaging" and analyzed stock on individual company fundamentals. In addition, through a portfolio of his own design, he sent three children through many, many years of college and graduate school.

My mother grew up in the Bronx, the daughter of a Jewish schoolteacher and an Irish nurse. She can remember the first of what would be a lifetime of teaching jobs, as a teenage camp counselor earning $60 for an entire summer of work. With that money, she bought a maple desk to have a place to do homework. My mother and father still have that desk.

While their kids were young, my parents had a functional partnership that was fairly traditional with respect to how they managed money. My father played monetary offense, being the primary earner, while my mother played monetary defense, managing the spending.

To this day, they agree on fundamental economic values, favoring thrift and prudence over waste and the purchase of luxury goods. They impressed upon us that what we did with our money was important, not just to our family, but to our community and the world at large. The companies in which my family members buy stock are those that make tangible products, create jobs and provide things the world needs. My brothers and I eventually stopped cringing every time my dad stopped to pick up litter to point out another product or company. We knew he wanted to share with us the good fortune of finding a Sweetheart® cup because we owned part of that company.

As I think back on those old family memories, I remember how I often felt embarrassed when my girlfriends came over to play Partridge Family albums. My dad would lecture us on the beauty of compound interest and give the girls annual reports of his favorite companies to take home. But the effect of that counsel is with us today. One childhood friend credits my father with her lifelong habit of saving ten percent of gross income for investments.

I took these socially functional and fairly common ideas about money into my own life's journey. In my teens and twenties I faced some tough challenges. From the outside my life looked successful. I received good grades, I was productive, and I easily conformed to social roles of student, worker and friend. But on the inside I did not have a strong sense of who I was as a person.

The only areas of my life that seemed to be stable were education, work and my personal finances. I was one of the few people in my group of friends for many years that had much money or any comfort level in using it, yet I was in pain. My emotional, physical and mental well-being suffered from my sense of disconnection to a greater reality, to a higher power. The feeling of grace I once felt as a young girl became covered over with anxiety, addictive habits and controlling behaviors. I was at a crossroads where more money, accomplishment or material things weren't going to fix the pain.

In my late twenties I joined support groups that introduced me to new concepts of spirituality. I reconnected with the essence of my earlier, more casual religious exposure and started on the path of a spiritual seeker. I cultivated a deep relationship to a greater reality than my past, my job, my roles or my stories. I rediscovered a power greater than myself. I came to understand that the grace that Sister spoke about is available to me in every area of my life.

I've now spent twenty plus years deeply involved in personal growth and spiritual expansion, while simultaneously creating worldly success in my profession as a corporate trainer and consultant. But for years I hid my competence in making and using money from my friends in the "spiritual world" as we shared our spiritual struggles. At the same time, I didn't reveal my emotional journey or my spiritual activities to my clients or colleagues in the "business world." I kept the two separate.

I soon learned that there's no reality in separation. My worlds were coming together. I enjoyed expense reports when the other consultants thought they were a pain because doing them was like a meditation to me. Before going in for a big presentation to our corporate buyers, I would silently bless everyone in the room. I delivered a seminar series on the stages of team development to groups in our spiritual community.

As I deepened in my spiritual practices, I became surprisingly comfortable seeing universal principles operating in financial matters and corporate life. As I developed expertise as a business consultant, I felt more confident about applying organizational effectiveness tools to the issues in my spiritual community.

In my life, I find that work, money, business, investments, meditation, prayer, spiritual study and God go together. My latest insights and experiences of integrating spirituality and money are the foundation of the message I'm sharing in *The Money Keys*.

What I know now is that there never was any good reason to hold money and spirituality as two separate areas of experience. Universal spiritual principles are compatible with the knowledge, actions and results of material success. It's possible to live a conscious, sacred life with a strong experience of inner guidance and connection to spiritual reality and, at the same time, to save, invest and share money effectively.

Today, I love God. God is my shorthand for the infinite, loving, ever-expanding, eternal nature of life. I feel God as a presence that is everywhere. God is at the heart of who I am.

Today, I also love playing the money game. This includes earning, spending, managing, giving and receiving money. I find the mathematics of accounting soothing and reliable.

My personal spiritual experiences concerning money and its meaning in my life have proven to me that integrating spirituality and worldly success is available to all. I'm committed to supporting clients, students and colleagues like you in achieving a vastly more inspiring and satisfying experience of money and its role in your life. My spiritual friends can enjoy more peace of mind and worldly success than they allow themselves to imagine. My entrepreneurial colleagues can have a greater connection to the power and possibility within their own souls.

What's the Money For?

A recent headline in *Newsweek* asked, "Does God Want You to Be Rich?" The article discusses the idea that in the area of financial matters, otherwise deeply religious and spiritual people aren't confident, connected or peaceful. The article extended that idea to individuals with creative natures, such as artists, writers and creative thinkers. Money makes them nervous. They quickly become uncomfortable when dealing with their finances.

The article also noted that this seems culturally counter-intuitive because Americans tend to view money, glamour, luxury and excess as desirable ends unto themselves. Who doesn't want to be a millionaire? It appears that more money is the key to happiness. But is that really so?

In writing this book, I used a spiritual practice called visioning, a practical tool I will teach you to apply to your financial life. It's the process of achieving a meditative state, aligning awareness with the infinite and intelligent presence of the divine, and then asking a series of questions to uncover the "vision" or uplifting spiritual qualities that are guiding and emerging in our lives.

My longtime prayer partner Jennifer and I enjoyed lunch one day overlooking the ocean in Manhattan Beach, California. Later, we engaged in a visioning session. During the visioning, the inspiration to write this book became clear to me. *The Money Keys* is dedicated to people who want to grow themselves as they grow their money. The entire book is about helping people find their own compelling answer to the question, "What's the money for?" In the vision, this book and I serve people who are not just interested in having more money for money's sake, but in having money contribute to more power, meaning and value in their lives.

There are a lot of innovative, lucrative and interesting money management and investment vehicles out there. Plenty of great real estate, wealth building and financial programs, and books and seminars sweep the country each year. This book is less about which investments to choose or programs to take and more about why you're choosing or taking them. *Why* are you trading in the foreign exchange market, for example? *Why* do you want to start a business? *Why* should you reduce your consumer debt, look for creative tax deductions or learn to day-trade? For security? Accumulation? World peace? Leaving a legacy? What does the money mean?

As a progressive, spiritually-minded wealth-builder, discovering your answer to the question, "What's the money for?" allows you to consciously create and share wealth in a way that empowers you and those around you.

The Opportunity Cost of Fear, Manipulation and Struggle

The financial term "opportunity cost" refers to the cost of passing up the next best choice when making a decision. To put it in monetary terms, for example, if you put $10,000 in a bond fund earning 7%, you have given up the opportunity to put $10,000 down on a piece of real estate. It's a useful measure for evaluating the trade-offs in your financial investments.

In the realm of our spiritual, mental and emotional experiences, the important currency that we invest is not money; it's our time, energy and attention. How we "invest" ourselves in time, energy and attention is the creator of our experience of life, money and ourselves.

There is an opportunity cost to investing yourself in worry, resentments and the frantic struggle to survive financially. When you're anxious, you can't feel any peace within yourself. When you're resentful, you don't feel free. When you are struggling, you're out of the flow. It's not that the timeless spiritual qualities of peace, freedom and expansion go away; you just don't feel and experience their power. When you make a decision to develop your spirituality, including your beliefs and habits around money, you are investing in peace, freedom and possibility, which are spiritual qualities that yield infinite returns.

Maximizing Your Investment in *The Money Keys*

The Money Keys is written for wealth-builders, investors, business people and entrepreneurs who want more depth, meaning and inner confidence in money. To get the most benefit from this book, I encourage you to be willing to start cultivating or expanding your own authentic spirituality, to get and stay financially organized, and to open up your heart and mind.

It's *Your* Spirituality

When I speak of spirituality, I refer to our relationship to the larger, creative, universal realities of life. Many people center their beliefs and practices on religion or God. Others concentrate on ethical values and a soulful nature, the aspect of life that is inner and invisible. The spirituality I speak of does not depend upon adherence to any particular religious tradition. In this book, we'll be working with universal principles that are found at the mystical essence of world religious traditions, ancient philosophies, and breakthroughs in the new ideas of science. I trust you to explore, discern, and adopt what information, ideas and practices within this book are most inspiring and relevant for you.

I believe that everybody has a "god" whether he or she is religious or not. When I say "god," I mean an understanding of a greater reality, a higher power or an organizing principle that underlies life itself. It could simply be the god of random evolution, a rational materialistic view of life, or "nothing." Your "god" also could be a deeply held religious doctrine with a deity to whom you have a strong relationship, and your life may be full of religious practices and belief.

If you have a rational, nonreligious worldview, I encourage you to incorporate the principles and practices offered here that feel relevant to you. If you have a strong religious doctrine and practices, I trust you'll select and practice the ideas and tools that support your faith. The intent is not to convert you or enroll you in anything. As you study the three universal spiritual principles and try out the twelve practices, I am confident that you'll develop a greater sense of what "god" means in your life.

Your Financial Foundation

For some of you, the practical financial information, suggestions, stories and tools may seem basic. They are. Establishing order in finances with good basic ideas is the foundation upon which to build a bigger, more powerful wealth game. Developing uplifting spirituality, mental empowerment, emotionally involving belief and highly effective habits are much easier when your basic financial structures are strong. The sophistication and subtleties lie in the universal spiritual principles, which are infinite and eternal.

The most powerful way to change is to be honest about where you are and to be clear about your destination. As you look to expand your financial wealth, having an accurate sense of where you're starting from is powerful. If you don't know how much money you have or owe, or where you've spent or invested it, implementing specific change will be hard. The basics that you'll need are a balance sheet of assets and liabilities, information about income from all sources, and current legal documentation of wills, trusts and family circumstances.

It is important for me to note that I don't know the details of your situation; therefore, I can't recommend specific financial actions. I am not a financial advisor or licensed in any way to make financial recommendations for you personally, nor is anything in the book to be construed as financial advice. The ideas presented are all for your spiritual, mental, emotional and behavioral education.

Chapter One

Real Financial Power

"Riches are not from abundance of worldly goods,

but from a contented mind."

– Mohammad

Chapter One

Open Your Mind and Heart

The ideas in *The Money Keys* are nothing new. I'm correlating wisdom from ancient, indigenous cultures of the East and West, New Thought spiritual concepts, and contemporary wealth-building ideas. I'm offering you my heartfelt commitment to your inherent abundance and well-being, as well as ideas and tools to complement what you may already "know" but have struggled to implement. The goal is to provide you with new ways of perceiving, thinking, feeling and acting around money and spirituality. If you maintain an open mind and heart, I guarantee you'll find something here to support your continued expansion and success.

Over the next few chapters, I'll lead you on a step-by-step path to discovering what money means in your life and how to find the peace, freedom and possibility you've only dreamed about!

The Doorway to Possibility

Imagine in your mind's eye a beautiful doorway. The door is made of material and constructed in a way that is inspiring and impressive to you. Behind that doorway, you are living the financial life of your dreams. Imagine that everything you have ever desired in regard to financial abundance is already yours. Picture yourself, and everyone who is important to you, enjoying the most expanded dream of wealth possible. See yourself as peaceful, free, joyous, generous, prosperous and powerful. Ahhhh...that image, that vision, that reality is our definition of real financial power.

As you step back into your present reality, close the beautiful door, but remember the image and experience of enjoying real financial power. Reflect on your image. Your highest desire or goal of wealth might have included a certain dollar amount, such as one million dollars. That's a common number that many aspire to. Or maybe ten million dollars or one hundred million dollars. But is that all?

For many people, our most inspiring image of wealth and prosperity is more than just frolicking in a pile of paper currency. The peace and freedom we enjoy in our dream emerges because of our underlying desire for how we'll use the money – what the money's for – and what having a great deal of money makes possible for us. At the highest level of prosperity, we are likely serving, sharing and doing things that reflect the best expression of who we are.

That's the doorway to real financial power. Power is the capacity to manifest, give, influence and reveal. Power that springs from our alignment with a higher power is not dominion, exploitation or control of others. When we access the vastness of who we are, we are generous, compassionate and cooperative.

Real power is an inner strength from which we connect with all of life. Marianne Williamson once said, "You were born to make manifest the glory of God. It's not just in some of us. It's in all of us."

This book is for people who are already interested and active in increasing their financial abundance. Generating more money can be an inspiring, courageous and high-integrity goal when you are aligned with your inner values, qualities and purpose.

Financially, real power can be expressed through the dollars that you have and how you share, spend, earn and save them. When you're in real financial power, your mind is clear, your emotions are at peace, your physical life is healthy and vital, and your relationships, projects, activities, profession and creativity are all expressing the best of who you are. Money in your life becomes another avenue for expressing the best of you. Money is not a limit or a constraint, but a tool. Real financial power includes faith, peace, choice and freedom.

Thus, the vision of a wealthy life is an individualized experience. We are not all standing at the same doorway surveying the same scene. For you, working in a career or profession that you enjoy with a home that's comfortable and spending time in nature with your animals might be your dream. For another person, real financial power might mean being a business mogul, living in a mansion and creating projects and businesses on a global scale.

Grow Your Money, Grow Yourself

Opening to your real financial power will cause you to grow in identity as well as grow your financial results. You will find the balance of action and reflection that's best for you.

Maybe you're already engaged in a multitude of reflective activities such as mediation, sharing, journaling and counseling. But when it comes to money, you have a lack of clear goals, financial knowledge or inspired actions. Too much reflection can create stagnation. You need to act.

Or you may have experienced money management programs that go to the other extreme of action, action, action. It's all about getting moving, staying moving and then moving some more. Action and accountability are the focus. But action without strong inner direction can feel frantic and exhausting. You need to incorporate reflection and integration with action and accountability.

The interrelationship between inner and outer, reflection and action can't be underestimated. There are natural cycles and rhythms throughout all of life. We sleep and wake. We inhale and exhale. As you grow yourself and grow your wealth, you may experience cycles of stillness and action.

Both reflective and active approaches to applying universal principles in spirituality, beliefs and habits are included at the end of the chapters in *The Money Keys*. Opportunities for reflection help you discover and strengthen your authentic interpretation of concepts. Taking new actions allows you to see, feel, hear and embody spiritual and financial tools. Many of you are familiar with the medical learning model of "see one, do one, teach one." We really know something when we are able to relate to it and apply it in our own lives.

Studying and applying spiritual principles leads to both evolutionary and transformative growth. Let me try to explain the difference between the two. Evolutionary growth is along a linear and incremental pattern of advancement. A baby crawls, then cruises, then walks. This happens in rather discreet stages across a one-directional timeline. The same is true in our financial lives. A young man gets a job at $25,000 a year, opens a 401(k), and hopes for annual raise in salary and shops for a car. This type of growth seems to be common sense, right? Indeed, our Western public education system is a good example of linear growth. The system builds upon each idea taught to a child, day-by-day, year-by-year, and eventually creates a knowledgeable individual.

In contrast, transformative growth operates differently from linear growth. Not only can we grow and change incrementally, but we can also grow by leaps and bounds. A scientist can observe this physical phenomenon through the study of quantum physics. Tiny particles orbit in predictable and observable patterns and then change orbit without appearing to move through time and space. This is referred to as a "quantum leap."

People can experience a quantum leap within themselves, called spiritual transformation. This is when we intuitively know something without having learned it in a step-by-step process. The pieces of a mental, physical or spiritual puzzle fit together in a way they never did before, giving us a moment of oneness and connection.

I've experienced both kinds of expansion as I surrender to what real financial power means for me. For six years I sold training and consulting services for a high-end boutique firm. I labored diligently to take care of my clients well. The second year I had a stellar sales year. After that, though, I struggled to exceed the sales quotas. The job required a fast-paced, gregarious approach that was challenging for me, and my enthusiasm waned. My belief at the time was that "money comes from hard work and struggle," and I was living with the effects of that belief.

I decided to leave my full-time role with the firm and become a subcontractor trainer. I taught workshops to firms on an as-needed basis. This was a good, linear move that included more flexibility and less stress for me. I had shifted to a more low-key position, but I hadn't shifted the underlying belief that money comes from hard work and struggle. Therefore, I ended up working hard at being free. Something was still missing.

Not until I committed to becoming an author, speaker and business owner while sharing my own message did I make my own quantum leap in spirituality, belief and habits. This new endeavor is built around the belief that "God is my source and anything is possible." I've had to surrender to a greater vision of radiance, truth-telling and inner guidance than ever before. I don't always know what the next steps are. I don't know how things are going to happen. I just know that I have said yes to something greater that's emerging. This is a leap into an unprecedented idea of who I am, creatively, professionally and financially.

As you come upon the doorway of real financial power in your life, there will be times for incremental linear growth and opportunities to surrender yourself to spiritual transformation.

Unlocking the Door

We all understand that the universe is a lawful place. Life, invisible and visible, operates on set principles or laws of being. Principles are truths that can be tested. Most people are familiar with the principles that exist in our physical world, such as the law of gravity. Physical laws are consistent, natural ways of being. The same is true of metaphysical laws, which are the laws that govern that which is beyond our visible, physical understanding.

The Money Keys is built upon three universal spiritual principles that describe the way all life works:

The Law of Unity

The Law of Unity is the universal principle of building a spirituality of wholeness. The Law of Unity says that all of life is connected to and created from one infinite, eternal source.

The Law of Cause and Effect

The Law of Cause and Effect is the way creation occurs. For every visible manifestation, there's an invisible idea behind it. Consciousness, which is the totality of thought, energy and belief, is the creative source of invisible ideas. As individuals, our consciousness is creative.

The Law of Circulation

The *Law of Circulation* is based on the spiritual idea that we live in an abundant, creative universe of infinite energy that is always flowing. The nature of life is giving and receiving.

Spiritual Practices

Studying and applying these laws can be a lifetime avocation. To assist you in living out these truths, I also present twelve practices that blend spiritual ideas with behaviors in physical world. These practices are as follows:

- *Gratitude*
- *Meditation*
- *Inspiration*
- *Visioning*
- *Inquiry*
- *Healing*
- *Co-creation*
- *Blessing*
- *Serving*
- *Spiritual giving*
- *Managing the Money Flow*
- *Your Wealth Expansion Plan*

Inspirational Stories

Throughout the book, I share stories of individuals who have been challenged to grow spiritually, mentally and emotionally in their relationship with money. I talk about how they changed their financial habits and the meaning money has in their lives. I hope you'll use the stories to stimulate ideas of what is possible for you.

The following story is about Martin, who has consciously chosen to push past social conditioning of what it means to be "poor," and even what it means to be "middle class." His vision of financial freedom for his new family requires him to stay faithful to his spirituality. He has used creative financing and built strong family habits in money-management to build a cohesive home life and a million-dollar real estate portfolio in three years.

Martin's Story

I was raised in a poor area. My mother received welfare and came from a long line of individuals who were poor. I absolutely believe my parents wanted the very best for me, but people can only teach to the extent of their own knowledge. I was conditioned to be poor by my upbringing and environment.

My first hurdle was overcoming my environment, which I did by getting a college education. I got my degree and landed a good job. When I started making decent money, I was like a child in a candy store with a paycheck, so I'd spend it all. I can remember in those early years thinking, "Man, I felt better off financially when I was a college student." The spending didn't make me rich. I was living a life of bondage to my conditioning.

By income standards I became middle-class, but by measure of net worth I was still poor because I couldn't manage my money well. The more I dug into my relationship with money, the more I saw a real lack of knowledge and understanding of how money worked. I was overcompensating when making that transition from being poor to middle-class. I felt a sense of entitlement. I spoiled myself with things, thinking that was what indicated success.

Then I became a young parent. I realized that I needed to do better, not just for myself but for future generations. I decided that my family legacy of poverty would stop with me. I knew it was not just about making more money to give to my children. This was about gaining a deeper knowledge and understanding about money to pass on to my children.

I transitioned into a new career in the real estate industry after being an engineer for just a couple of years, which took a great deal of faith. During my first year in the real estate business, I struggled financially. I didn't make much money. I racked up a significant amount of debt.

I was committed to fulfilling my wife's desire to be a stay-at-home mom. We were relying on my income, which was not predictable or steady. We had a new baby in the house that required all the things that babies need. I moved my family into a 400 square foot converted garage. In our studio there was one room that was our bedroom. It was also our living room and the nursery - and my home office.

I remember my first year vividly because it was an important and very difficult year. I had not been responsible with money in the past, and I know now that if I had attained success in the real estate business right away, the money would have flowed through my hands right away.

I believe God has plans for us all, but we must have integrity as human beings for God to fulfill those plans. One of the sacred stories I like is the story of Joseph. Early in his life God gave him premonitions about great plans. Joseph was tested; he became a prisoner and a slave. But he stayed faithful to God. When he was a prisoner, he was a good prisoner. Eventually, he was free to fulfill his life's purpose. His faith throughout his challenges is an inspiration to me.

   I value the education I received through the hardship of that first year. I maintained a certain level of integrity when it came to money. My creditors got paid before I put food on the table. I remember the twelfth month, when I had only a couple thousand dollars left in my checking account and my credit cards were all maxed out. It was the end of the line, and there were many things I could have done that would not have been faithful.

   I could have crawled back to another job as an engineer and said, "I tried and I failed. It just didn't work out" and dismissed the whole effort. It would have been perfectly acceptable, and plenty of people would have agreed with me. I also could have decided that I wasn't going to pay my creditors that month, that I'd rather keep the money for myself. Instead, I was faithful in my commitment that wherever I was in my life was exactly where God wanted me to be. When I borrowed the money, I agreed to pay those creditors back according to certain terms, and so I did.

   The very next month, more money came into my life that covered my debts and obligations. From there I was able to pull out of the financial hole. It was very much a test of faith. Looking back on the last four years, everything had to happen exactly that way for me to be where I am today. When I look at most hardships and struggles in people's lives, I have the opportunity to really learn about faith. I stayed faithful and maintained integrity with other people and passed the test.
My integrity with people and money actually came from my mother. If she owed you a dollar, she would hunt you down to give you your dollar back. Early on my mother struggled. She didn't have an education, and she always worked low-wage jobs. Even on a little bit of money, she managed to own her life, for the most part, free and clear. Her home is paid off.

Money is about freedom and nothing more. It buys the freedom to do the things that I want to do. My financial ambition is to pay off my future free and clear.

I went from 400 square feet of living space to 4,000 square feet. At the lowest point in the first year, I was down to my last penny and had $40,000 in personal debt on top of my house payment and car payment. Now, three years later, I'm officially a millionaire. I believe God has plans for us all, but we have to have integrity as human beings for God to fulfill those plans.

Your Turn

Martin has a faithful belief and persistent approach to greater possibility in his financial life. The choice to create freedom and growth for himself and his family is the foundation of his decisions and actions. Martin is discovering the spirituality, beliefs and habits that are best suited to his journey. Now it's your turn.

Chapter One Review

Questions for Reflection

1) What do I want to get out of reading The Money Keys?

2) How do I best balance action and stillness in learning and growing?

Ideas for Action

1) Write your Money Story. Knowing where you've come from and where you want to go with money is powerful. You may want to begin a new journal for your The Money Keys practices or just start with a blank paper or screen. You're going to capture facts, feelings, and the role of faith. When you've completed your story, you might share it with a prosperity partner, a loved one, friend or coach for the purpose of appreciating where you've been and seeing how it relates to where you're going. In order to create your own story, start with the following questions.

What are the facts? Find, research or estimate the answers to these questions:

- What was the financial status of my family growing up?

- What was our net worth when I was born, as a teen and today?

- How much income did my parents make over time and from what sources?

- What have been the major money events of my life, including marriage, divorce, inheritance, jobs, bonuses, business, real estate, bankruptcy, investments, etc.?

- As an adult, what's the largest amount of money and the least amount of money I've made in a year?

- Right now, what are the important facts of my financial life?

What are the feelings?

For this section, write your story in the first person ("I felt thrilled when we finally had our own home") or write your story as fiction ("There once was a little boy who wanted to be a businessman like his dad, but he loved to paint and draw.")

Answer these questions:

- What did it feel like to talk about, spend, save, share or invest money in my home as a child, a teen and a young adult?

- What do I remember feeling and thinking about money? Use "feeling words," such as excited, jealous, happy, worried, mystified, calculating, and so forth.

- For the big money events of my life, what feelings and memories are associated with them?

Where was the faith?

- What, if any, religious or spiritual connections were there in my past regarding money and its role in my life?

Tools

Visit **www.themoneykeys.com/tools** to join our mailing list to receive the latest version of *The Money Keys Resources*, a list of books, services, education and tools as well as regular emails with ideas, stories, tips and offers for developing your spirituality, beliefs and habits around money and its meaning in your life.

Chapter Two

Escaping the Money Traps

"The trouble with being poor is that

it takes up all your time."

– Willem De Kooning

What Is Money?

Dictionaries commonly define money as "the current medium of exchange." That's it!

Money is a tool for facilitating the exchange of goods and services in an orderly manner. Money acts as a vehicle for giving and receiving "things" that have worth or value to the parties involved in the exchange. We imbue money, which is the symbol, with its meaning. We etch meaning into money with our beliefs about it. We trust that a little green piece of paper labeled $10 gives us the power to buy things. We agree to this as we're purchasing our lattes, paying the power company or contributing to charities.

Indeed, money is involved in many of the things that define who we are and the things we do. It is a pervasive symbol of exchange between buyers and sellers, parents and children, and bosses and employees. Money is a method for communicating value.

In fact, wealth educator Loral Langemeier states that "[m]oney may not be the most important thing in your life, but it's certainly the most impactful." She uses a good analogy. Most of us could stop physical exercise for a couple of months, and our lives and well-being would not be too negatively affected. After a while, we might be able to start getting ourselves back in physical shape. But think about living without money for sixty days. Most of us simply couldn't do it. On a physical, practical level, money is a regular necessity for living.

What Money Means

Money symbolizes something to each one of us. That something is its meaning in our lives. I'm using the word "meaning" to capture our entire framework of ideas, thoughts, feelings and responses in how we interpret, relate to and encounter life. Meaning is our view of ourselves and the world. Meaning is not neutral. It is our perceived reality. Our meaning creates our experience of reality.

Of course, there isn't one objective, ultimate reality in life. There are phenomena of experience and the meanings we make out of them, and money is not immune to this process. In fact, many people attach more intense emotion, superstition and unrealistic ideas to money than to almost any other area of their lives. The reason this is important to understand is that we are choosing the meaning we attach to our financial lives. We choose. This also means we can change that meaning into anything we want, but we must believe that we have the power to do so.

So, what we believe is what we experience. We are the ones who look upon a beautiful sunset and make the decision that the world is a friendly place. Or we may look upon a beautiful sunset and decide that, because we aren't holding the hand of the perfect romantic partner, nothing really matters.

We have the power to choose our reactions, interpretations, attitudes and responses to life and create the meaning that we want out of our experiences. When we know this, we have access to unlimited choice. That's the purpose of this book: to equip individuals with alternative, positive, empowering, inspiring ways to change their ideas and attitudes about money.

In our financial lives, external situations happen or don't happen the way we would like them to. Take an event, for example, such as a client's check bouncing. It happened, and it affected you. The meaning and the experience you attach to the situation is up to you. You could feel a rush of adrenaline and make an angry phone call, or you could assume a computer error and calmly hand the matter back to your bookkeeper for follow-up. What you do with what happens is *meaning* management, and it is as important as *money* management. The meaning you choose profoundly affects your sense of spiritual well-being, mental and emotional balance, as well as your capacity to take inspired actions in your life.

We give money the power to bring overwhelming peace or utter chaos to our lives. The green paper, the metal discs and the digits on the screen have only the power and meaning we assign them. When our financial circumstances become thoughts and feelings of constraint, threat or suffering, we have fallen into a money trap.

The Money Traps

Scarcity

Each of us has a primary belief about the nature of the universe and why life is the way it is. Every aspect of our lives reflects that reality. We serve our view of reality through investing our time, energy, attention and resources. We all serve a reality in our money lives. The spectrum of spiritual reality ranges from scarcity, alone on the desert island, to the divine reality of wholeness, at one with all of life.

Thus, the first money trap we can fall into is **scarcity**. Scarcity feels like a storm has left us stranded on a desert island all alone. We feel fear when we allow ourselves to view money from the specter of scarcity.

Much of the collective behavior in Western culture concerning money is based on scarcity. It's a subtle yet pervasive assumption that there are just not enough resources to go around. When you place your energy and attention on that assumption, it's no wonder you feel persistent anxiety about money! When you're afraid of not having enough, you withhold, you hoard, you constrict.

Scarcity is the anxiety-ridden idea of lack. You feel there is a lack of money, time, resources, deals, creativity, people and supply. Where there is scarcity, there is fear, anxiety, worry, tension, hoarding, hiding and withholding. Many of the individual, group and global conflicts in life result from the idea of scarcity.

Unfortunately, on a global level, humans are not successfully circulating the infinite energy available to us so that all people have their basic needs met. We suffer as a planet when some are caught up in over-consuming and others starve. Both extremes of empty materialism and starvation are outer expressions of the shadow of scarcity.

The key question to ask to break the spell of scarcity around money is "What reality am I serving?" By "reality," I mean spiritual worldview. This is not necessarily just a religious view, but the individual understanding and definition of transcendent reality, a higher power or creative source.

The reason the spell of scarcity must be broken is because scarcity is a lie. The damage done by the lie of scarcity happens when you believe there's not enough and act accordingly. When you act from scarcity, you serve the idea of lack. You organize your decisions and choices in a way to maximize your good while someone else goes without.

If you are pursuing wealth for protection or security alone, and you're operating in the shadow of scarcity, then you can have a sense of emptiness. Someone who's very fearful may be able to generate money, but no amount of money will ever really address the challenge of scarcity. *Fear is a faith issue, not a financial one.*

You see, scarcity is a horrible reality to serve. It will always remind you that there's not enough and that you're not enough. No amount of activity or material results can appease the idea of scarcity.

In contrast, serving a reality of wholeness in our financial lives means we celebrate the reality that the universe is for us. Wholeness means that life is fundamentally intelligent, creative and complete. Faith in wholeness assures us that no matter the circumstances, there is a presence for good that supplies us.

The universal spiritual principle that underlies wholeness is *The Law of Unity*. This is the first money key. The *Law of Unity* says that all of life is connected to and created from one infinite, eternal source. When you believe that you are at one with your creative source, you can find your authentic answer to "What's the money for?" The practices of gratitude, meditation, inspiration and visioning that you'll learn in chapter four will help you cultivate your realization of this truth. When we serve a reality of wholeness, we don't feel alone on our desert island. We realize that a higher power than our experience and circumstances is our creative source, and when we realize that, we feel peace. With an uplifting financial spirituality based in wholeness, we're more balanced, centered and grateful.

The secret to permanent peace of mind is not a dollar amount. It's not a getting a lover or a job or an investment to give you more. It's choosing to serve a reality of wholeness rather than the specter of scarcity. When we know that wholeness is our source, we can be at peace. We're rescued from that lonely island.

Superstition

The next money trap is **superstition**. Superstition feels like "they" have unjustly given you a life sentence behind bars. Something out there is making you mad. You're angry or resentful about your ex, the IRS, the boss, your family, yourself. You don't feel good about money. You don't feel good about not having it, or you don't feel good about giving it away. Superstitions are mentally disempowering and emotionally draining concepts that don't serve your wealth or your well-being.

Superstitions come from misguided beliefs. Beliefs are mental thoughts combined with emotional reactions, held in place by repetition and intensity. In your financial lives, your superstitious beliefs of being victimized or fighting about money operate in your current conscious minds and in your subconscious, where you've been conditioned to believe certain ideas about money.

Superstitions around money show up as phrases such as "money is bad," "money is hard," and "money is out of my control." Superstitions are ideas that often don't stand up to logic or scrutiny. The idea that money is bad includes the feeling that money is dirty, difficult, inherently compromising or not spiritual. This idea is particularly painful if you feel a sense of spiritual connection and believe in a loving and plentiful universe, while struggling to pay the rent because "my work doesn't pay well" or some other subtle superstition.

There's a superstitious idea that spirituality implies poverty. As a minister, I've been asked many times, "Why does the church charge for classes, counseling and events?" If I were a housekeeper, mechanic or doctor, would people ask me why there's a charge for services? Is being spiritual an agreement to be separate from money?

Another superstition is "money is hard." It's the notion that getting, keeping, living with and understanding money is difficult. Money is a tough game with winners and losers, and time is always running out. In wealth-building projects and workshops with investors, network marketers, corporate professionals and entrepreneurs, I find that people sometimes feel trapped in the pursuit of winning. The belief is that cutthroat competition, "more, faster, harder" is the only way to get ahead and get things done.

The idea that "money is controlled by others" is a superstition that sets up a situation with victims and perpetrators. You'll know if you harbor this superstition if you have blame, resentment or guilt in your money relationships. Are you complaining about the Internal Revenue Service, the ex, your boss, your family, the market or the corporations?

The key question to ask to escape the mental and emotional prison of superstition is "What game am I playing?" Remember that money is just a symbol; it has no power other than the meaning we give it. The money game can be played along a full spectrum from control to co-creation. Are you using money to dominate and exploit people and opportunities? Do you view competition as winning at the expense of others? That's a money game of control based on superstition. Or are you playing the game of collaboration, choosing to give your time, energy and attention in exchange for value, thereby creating more good for all? That's a game of co-creation.

The second money key is *The Law of Cause and Effect*. It shows how our consciousness, the sum total of our thought, feeling and belief, is creative. Our beliefs about money are directly related to our money experience. Identifying and shifting beliefs is a process using the practices of inquiry, healing and co-creation. These practices, described in chapter five, show you how to journal, work with a coach, and forgive, as well as apply affirmation, prayer and ritual in building new beliefs about money, you, and the game that you want to empower.

The people you choose to have around you are your money models, mirrors and mentors. All of them powerfully affect your money experience. The issue of control is solved with the insight that you choose your companions, beliefs, energy and ultimately your experience of money. That means you have freedom. You come out of the trap of superstition into the game of creativity! With this understanding, you're more present. You access your strengths. No longer a victim or a dominator, you take responsibility for choosing a game of creativity where everybody benefits. The game is now win/win.

Do you want true financial freedom that can never be controlled by others? It's not a dollar amount. You won't find it in real estate or foreign exchange or network marketing. True financial freedom is found in developing a mentally empowering and emotionally involving belief system around money that is all about the game of creation. It's the "get out of jail free forever" card.

Survival Mode

The final money trap is **survival mode**. You blew it, wandered off track and got stuck in quicksand, and now you flail around, exhausted but still stuck. There are times when your money habits feel like defense and survival. Trying to prevent bad things from happening is not an inspiring way to live. You feel self-centered, out-of-balance and unfulfilled.

Survival mode can feel like working hard but getting nowhere. Some suffer in their financial lives because of a lack financial education or technical knowledge of economics, accounting, investing and mathematics, areas necessary to be successful in managing, investing and growing financial wealth. Developing financial knowledge is essential and possible for those who want to have a different experience with money.

The key question to ask is "How am I growing?" When you treat your financial life as a place to learn, grow and expand the best of who you are in order to share your gifts with the world, everybody wins. That's thriving, not surviving. You line up your habits around money to serve a reality of wholeness and play a game of creation, whatever your circumstances.

The *Law of Circulation* shows us that all of life is a flow of giving and receiving. This is the third money key. When you engage in the practices presented in chapter six, including blessing, serving and spiritual giving, you get into that flow consciously. Do you want to immediately feel more prosperity in your life? It's not going to come from winning a prize, marrying a millionaire, or getting lucky. Feeling prosperous comes from a grateful attitude, a generous heart and a life of circulation. Start giving your thanks, your blessings, and your treasures. See how powerful it is to receive in kind.

Learning the practice of managing the money flow with the intention to thrive is vital, as is building an expansion plan of personal growth. If you wanted to improve your physical health, you might have to learn more about how your body works. You would eat nutritious food, exercise and care for yourself. If you wanted to hike the Himalayas, you would need to become educated about how to do it and have the right equipment, guidance and physical training to accomplish this goal. If you wanted to learn French, you would have to study and practice it. If you want to move into a more powerful, affluent and effective experience in your financial life, you must learn, grow and expand your skills, knowledge and financial capacity.

When you focus on thriving and growing rather than just surviving, you stop struggling. Out of the trap of survival, you feel that you're "in the flow." You connect with infinite possibility for yourself and your money life. You'll be lifted up out of the quicksand and onto the path of expansion.

Spirituality, Beliefs and Habits

The solutions to address scarcity, superstition and survival require a commitment to build an integrated connection between your financial and spiritual life, one that is spiritually uplifting, mentally empowering and emotionally involving. It also involves growing your knowledge and skills and developing mastery in financial habits. Choosing new meaning about money in your life and creating new results means you must serve a reality of wholeness, play a game of co-creation, and choose to thrive and grow.

By asking the three key questions and cultivating your practice of the *Law of Unity*, the *Law of Cause and Effect*, and the *Law of Circulation*, you can escape the money traps and create a financial life that is in alignment with what's true about life, money and you.

The ultimate truth about life is that we live in a loving universe. Each of us is whole and made from wholeness. There's plenty of everything available because the source of energy we are created out of is infinite. We are free to choose our responses to life and to experience the meaning of our mental and emotional choices. With infinite intelligence flowing through us, we can create games where everybody wins. Because we are ever expanding, there is always more to learn, more to express and more potential to fulfill.

This approach involves time, energy, attention and resources. Developing spirituality, beliefs and habits around money and its meaning is enhanced through the principles and practices you will learn in this book. However, you can't just say the spiritual words without feeling the pain of superstitious beliefs and healing them. You can't just change your habits and get busy if you don't have a reality of wholeness and believe in a game where you're free to choose.

Therefore, if you have a great deal of credit card debt, you may need both a spiritual realization of your wholeness *and* a specific plan to pay it off. If you have few financial assets and want to have the option to leave your job, you may need to trust the divine *and* start an investment program. If you have a significant amount of money but feel a surge of terror when you're asked to give to charity, you may need to start automatic charitable giving *and* deal with your anxiety.

You can be and do what's needed to unlock the doorway and step into your experience of peace of mind, freedom of choice, infinite possibility, and real financial power. This is true for you right now. Regardless of how much you have or owe, where the money is or isn't, or what your circumstances look like, you can expand beyond scarcity, superstition and survival mode.

Don't Look to the Culture to Know Your Value

In our culture, some people have made a psychological error in mixing up inner qualities of value and worth with outer measures of consumption and glamour. We might *say* as a culture that we value teachers and firefighters, but we *pay* more to movie stars and ball players. The culture is out of balance. You are probably familiar with the concept that the rich get richer and the poor get poorer. Indeed, the Census Bureau reports that 32.9 million Americans (11.7%) now live in poverty, and the Federal Reserve also reports that 71% of all assets are currently owned by only 10% of the population.

If you rely on outer standards of money measurement to compare and track your worth, you get lost. Comparison is a downward spiral of disempowerment. Making judgments about value based only on external factors can have you infer unreal things about yourself, your loved ones and others.

Wendy Jaffe, author of *The Divorce Lawyers' Guide to Staying Married*, states that the third most common reason people divorce is money. A survey by the National Depression Campaign found that financial problems were cited by 88% of the responders as a trigger for depression. And these problems aren't just confined to the United States. A report by the National Academic Press in Japan indicated that 28.7% of all suicides there are money related.

Spiritually, your value is your intrinsic worth, based on who you are from the inside out, not on what you do, what you own or what roles you play. You are created out of infinite, eternal reality, and your essential nature is more than your body, personality and portfolio. Making the commitment to learn, practice and live from the spiritual principles and practices of *The Money Keys* is a form of celebrating your intrinsic worth, claiming your true value, and living your authentic expression of wealth. Your value is priceless, just by you being who you are!

When you choose to celebrate your inherent value and to create new ideas about money that are in alignment with wholeness, co-creation and thriving, then you are making an important contribution to more than just yourself. Everything you do in your spiritual, business, personal and community lives is connected.

And if you turn away from the reality of scarcity and serve wholeness, then you are contributing more wholeness to all. If you choose to release the superstitions of dominance and competition and play a money game of co-creation, you are sharing more creativity for all. When you move beyond survival mode and develop habits of mastery and expand your knowledge, you're helping others to thrive. This is true, regardless of the roles you play, the jobs you have, the amounts you circulate, or any other external measure.

There's a Pony in Here Somewhere!

Now I would like to illustrate these truths with a short little tale. Twin girls, Positive-Little-Karen and Not-So-Positive-Little-Karen, wake up on their tenth birthday and are told there's a present for them in the barn. They rush out only to discover a large pile of manure. The Not-So-Positive twin complains about never getting anything good, but the Positive twin claps her hands and says, "There's a pony in here somewhere!"

This pony story is a classic example of the power you have to choose meaning. In your financial life, you may be confronted with what looks like that pile of manure, but you get to choose whether or not to find the pony.

Years ago, I made an investment that, at the time, was new to me but had the best returns I'd ever heard of. I thought I checked it out well enough and could trust the team involved. The investment made solid gains as promised for two years, and I was quite proud of myself.

In the third year, the storms came, and I felt stranded on the desert island. Not only did the returns stop, but the entire project and my principal were at risk. It sure *looked* like a pile of manure. I got upset and couldn't see the lesson the experience contained. I just felt angry. Really angry. As I obsessed about the time and money lost, every hurt, injustice, disrespect and wrong turn of my life replayed in my mind. As I worried about the details, people and decisions involved, my feelings of fear, blame and guilt were exacerbated. I also engaged in frantic actions to try to change things. I was serving scarcity, playing a game of financial victim, and struggling to survive.

It took a little while for me to realize what was happening. I'd had a breakdown in my own integrity on every level including my actions, decisions, thoughts, emotions and spiritual serenity. Restoring myself to balance was critical.

I had forgotten that I am one with the infinite, eternal, creative source. I was giving over my peace of mind to a channel through which the infinite flows. But my connection to the source is not dependent on anything external.

Immediately I focused my spiritual practice on reconnecting with my wholeness, starting with gratitude. I prayed and meditated for my own peace and realization of the wholeness and integrity of everyone involved.

I had to look at my superstitious beliefs contributing to the mental and emotional mindset that got me into this investment in the first place. I didn't fully ask the questions, do the research, or trust my gut with early red flags. I jailed myself with the idea that I didn't want to miss out or this deal might pass me by. Through journaling and working with a spiritual counselor, I inquired into my beliefs about myself, my self-worth and my ability to speak up. I wrote long letters releasing the anger and hurt and fear, which I read to my prosperity partner and burned. I forgave the individuals involved, especially myself, for the judgments I held. I looked for the lessons that could be learned through this experience.

I've also changed my behavior in managing the flow of money and developed new habits in my decisions, research, and investment choices. I needed to grow in the area of due diligence, which is a process for evaluating financial investments. I've built my capacity to ask better questions about projects and get input from a variety of people. I took conscious actions to complete my time with this project and this team, blessing all and moving on.

I found the pony! This situation has been a place to experience all the elements of *The Money Keys*: the money traps, the key questions, the universal spiritual laws, and the practices of spirituality, beliefs and habits. I also feel humbled. I appreciate the necessity of continuously developing my own spiritual strength, empowering beliefs, and greater mastery in my money habits.

Chapter Two Review

Questions for Reflection

1) What does money mean to me?

- Take a blank piece of paper and write "Money" at the top.

- On one side of the paper write the phrase "Money is." Spend five full minutes writing, without stopping or editing, your thoughts, feelings and words to complete the phrase "Money is..."

- On the other side of the paper write the phrase "Money is not." Spend five full minutes writing, without stopping or editing, your thoughts, feelings and words to complete the phrase "Money is not..."

- When you're done, read what's written. Any surprises? Share your insights with a prosperity partner, coach or friend.

2) Do I see myself as the meaning maker or as a victim of circumstances in my financial life?

3) What do I feel, think and know about my inherent value, beyond what I do and the roles I play?

Ideas for Action

1)   Take a field trip to discover more about your spiritual, mental and emotional views about money, value, "others," and you. Over a one week period, make two trips, one to an environment that represents "poor" to you and one to an environment that represents "rich." For "poor," you could serve a meal at a homeless shelter, work on a clean-up or service project, or sit in a bus station. For "rich," you could visit an art gallery, the finest hotel in town, or an expensive shopping area. Spend at least one hour in each location, interacting with people, with the following questions in your heart and mind.

- What reality is being served here - scarcity or wholeness? How do I know? What evidence, feeling or information am I using?

- What's true about the intrinsic value of people as individuals? Can I see or sense the unity or connection of life regardless of circumstances?

- How do I really feel about myself, my value, my place?

Tools

Visit **www.themoneykeys.com/tools** to listen to the audio mini-course *Escaping the Money Traps*.

Chapter Three

Your Money Map

"The use of money is all the advantage
there is in having money."

– Benjamin Franklin

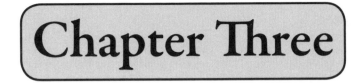

Chapter Three

We've looked at the challenges of the money traps, identified the key questions to ask to get you moving toward escaping the traps, and introduced the three spiritual laws and twelve spiritual practices. All of these elements are part of the journey of growth that includes developing your spirituality, beliefs and habits that leads to living the wealthy, prosperous, generous life that is uniquely yours to live.

The money map allows you to see all of these elements in one place. When you can see what's going on, you can both celebrate where you are now and dream about what's possible for you! Your money map is a framework for everything you will need for being, doing and having what you want in your inner and outer financial life.

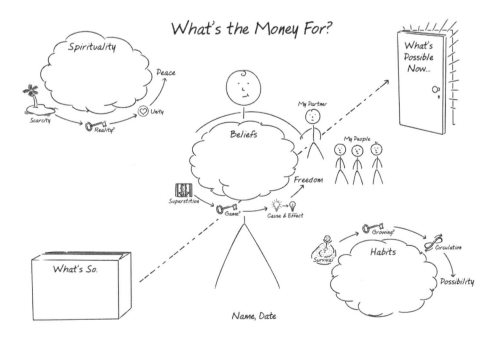

The money map shows the link between what's so in your money life and the doorway to what's possible. The link is you...your spirituality, belief and habits, as well as the partner and the people with whom you choose to share your money life.

In spirituality, we see the trap of scarcity represented by the desert island, and the key question to ask is, "What reality am I serving?" The area of spirituality is organized around the principle of the *Law of Unity*. The practices to grow spirituality are gratitude, meditation, inspiration and visioning. The result of cultivating an uplifting spirituality around money is peace.

In beliefs, we see the trap of superstition represented by the jail cell, and the key question to ask is, "What game am I playing?" The area of beliefs is focused around the principle of the *Law of Cause and Effect*. The practices to strengthen beliefs are inquiry, healing and co-creation. The outcome of developing mentally empowering and emotionally involving money beliefs is freedom.

In habits, we see the trap of survival represented by the quicksand, and the key question to ask is, "How am I growing?" The area of habits is connected to the principle of the *Law of Circulation*. The practices to build conscious habits are blessing, serving, spiritual giving, managing the money flow, and wealth expansion plan. Engaging in conscious financial habits leads to the realization of infinite possibility.

Create Your Money Map

Begin by drafting your customized version of a money map. You can draw the map as we go through the instructions below, or you can read the instructions and the whole chapter and then create your map.

- Take a piece of paper.
- Turn it sideways into the "landscape" position.
- Using a dark pencil or pen, in the center of the page, draw a stick figure of yourself leaving space above and below you.
- Write your name and today's date at the bottom of the page.
- In the bottom left corner of the page, draw a box about one inch square and label it with the words, "What's So."
- Underneath "What's So," put the relevant numeric facts of your money life. Choose numbers that are good shorthand for you to depict the current facts of your money life.
- Write your net worth (the difference between your assets and liabilities).
- Write your current monthly or yearly income.
- In the upper right corner of the paper, draw a doorway with a knob on it about two inches tall, leaving some space around and beyond the door. Label the door with the words, "What's Possible Now."
- Draw a dotted line from the bottom left corner of the page diagonally up to the upper right corner. The dotted line will go right through you in the center of the page.

Moving from what is so in your life into a larger idea and manifestation of what is possible is a movement through you. As you add the elements of spirituality, beliefs and habits, you'll see they are aspects of you that contribute to creating your life. Leave the area of "What's Possible Now" that is behind the door open for now.

- On the upper left hand side of the page, draw a cloud with about an inch and a half of space inside it. Label the top of the cloud "Spirituality."
- Move to the center of the page. Across your heart area in the stick figure, draw a similar cloud and label it "Beliefs."
- Move to the bottom right hand corner of the page. On the right side of your feet, draw another cloud and label it "Habits."

Your spirituality is represented by that aspect of you that is connected to a higher power. This higher power is a larger reality found within us and beyond us. We've placed spirituality "above" to represent an expanded realm, not necessarily a location. The divine may be symbolized by humanity's looking upwards, toward Father Sky, or by looking at the "god" in Mother Earth. The map has you put the area of beliefs not just in the head. This is because beliefs are active in our conscious minds, but they are also active in our emotions and in our physical bodies. And you represent the area of habits near your feet because actions connect you to the physical world.

Now go deeper into the content of your spirituality, beliefs and habits:

- In the realm of spirituality, ask yourself, "What reality am I serving in my money life now?" You can write the phrase "Reality?" on the money map under the spirituality area as shorthand.

- Do you have fears of scarcity or lack, anxieties about your place and safety in the greater reality of life? What can you be sure of about God or spirit or higher power? What is the dominant tone of your faith? Jot down a few words or phrases that capture the nature of your spirituality.

- In the realm of beliefs, ask yourself right now, "What game am I playing in my financial life?" You can write the phrase "Game?" on the money map under the beliefs area as shorthand.

- What, if any, superstitious beliefs do you have about yourself, money and what it means, how life works, or what others have control over? Are you angry, resentful, depressed or guilty about money? What money issues take up your mental and emotional attention?

- Are there empowering beliefs about collaboration and cooperation that are active for you? Do you have a sense of hope, excitement, joy and generosity around money, the projects and work you're doing, and the people with whom you're doing them? Jot down a few words or phrases that capture the nature of your beliefs.

- In the realm of habits, ask yourself, "How am I growing in my money life?" You can write the phrase "Growing?" on the money map under the habits area as shorthand. Are you struggling to survive? Are you frantically busy? Do you handle your debts, bills or responsibilities with integrity? Can you access information or resources that you need to pay your bills, build for the future and create the life you want? Are you inspired when it comes to earning and using money? Are you financially generous? Do you have goals, plans, investments and a process for managing your money? Jot down a few words or phrases that capture the nature of your habits.

Now add a few more elements to your map:

- On the right side of the page, draw a single stick figure, perhaps holding your hand, to represent your partner if you have or desire a significant romantic or business partner with whom you share your money life.

- Draw a few figures and label them "Your People," to represent your current or desired inner circle of family, friends, co-workers or community members.

- Take a moment to consider the major theme of your relationship with your partner and your people concerning money, and then add a symbol, word or phrase next to your partner and your people that captures that theme. It could be something like, "launching the business," "sharing the ride," "the Hatfield's and the McCoy's," or whatever means something to you.

So far you've created a money map that represents your money experience up until this present moment, characterized by the phrase, "What's So." You likely have a sense of what you would like to shift, change and grow in your money life. So now switch to a different colored pen, pencil or marker, and move to the area of "What's Possible Now."

"What's Possible Now" includes the spirituality, beliefs, and habits you know you'd like to learn, develop or create. And "What's Possible Now" includes the yet-to-be-revealed aspects of your infinite, eternal, abundant nature.

- Start in the upper right hand corner of the page, behind and around the door, and doodle in the words, phrases or symbols of your best idea of what's possible in your money life. It could be a dollar amount, a graduation cap that represents your toddler finishing law school, or a single phrase like Martin's "Owning my future free and clear."

For you to move into what's possible, you will need to engage your spirituality, beliefs and habits.

- Move around your map, and add two to three elements of what needs to emerge for you in spirituality, beliefs, and habits.

- In spirituality, for example, you might desire more communion with unconditional spiritual qualities such as wholeness, order, power, truth, peace, love or joy.

- In beliefs, for example, you might capture the desire to heal your resentment of a certain person, forgive yourself or release judgments. The beliefs area would also be the place to capture the emotional qualities that you want to choose in your work, creativity and projects, such as freedom, joy and collaboration.

- In habits, you could note specific actions you aspire to take, such as financial giving to spiritual causes and institutions, better money management, a commitment to learning about real estate, paying off debts, etc.

- Using the pen or pencil you are now using for "What's Possible Now," capture anything you know needs to grow and expand about your partner or your people. It could be something like "sharing goals," "making a difference," or "expanding my network."

- Take a moment to look over your money map. See if there are any other things you want to include under "What's Possible Now" and write them in.

Take a deep breath. Does this money map include all the big ideas, thoughts, feelings, actions and facts that are important in your financial life? If not, add anything you need to. When you know it's complete, congratulate yourself! You have in front of you a simple way to see the major elements of your money life.

Now write across the top of your money map, "What's the Money For?" Your spirituality, beliefs and habits around money are creating something. Your life is "for" something. The money map lets you see what the money's for in your life.

Now that you know where you are, you can choose to focus on the specific areas of change that are most relevant to you in your money life.

Time Is on Your Side

Notice that the money map doesn't include much information on where you have been. The past is over, except for the energy, attention and time you give it in the present. Your past can be a source of wisdom, insight and power, depending on whether you choose to learn from past experiences. The results you have in your life right now are the evidence of the reality you've been serving, the games you've been playing, and the survival skills you've been using. The emphasis here is on growing from where you are into what you can be.

Celebrating What's So and Welcoming What's Possible

In many ways the money map is a snapshot of the inner and outer aspects of your financial life. A financially and spiritually sophisticated individual can feel the interconnectedness of spirituality, life purpose and money. Your attitude toward yourself is a powerful determinant of your capacity to flourish. Find what is positive about your story, your consciousness and your circumstances, and celebrate it.

In an ever-expanding universe, there are always more aspects of our inner nature and capacities to be revealed. If there are things in your money life that aren't working, know that you have the power to change your experience through your spirituality, beliefs and habits. The possibilities of spiritual inspiration, mental empowerment, emotional balance and conscious actions in your money life are limitless, no matter what the circumstances of your life are. I encourage you to dream big about the peace of mind, sense of freedom and experience of possibility available to you. The coming chapters are all designed to go deeper into what's possible for you in spirituality, beliefs, habits, partnership, people and more.

Next Steps with Your Map

There are many ways to continue working with and using the money map. A completed map helps you to know which of the upcoming chapters on spirituality, beliefs and habits may be most important for you to focus on in *The Money Keys*. The process of creating your money map can become a regular meditative exercise, and you can use the audio tools at **www.themoneykeys.com** to guide you through it. You can meet with a coach or prosperity partner or work in a mastermind team, a group of individuals dedicated to learning and growing in wealth knowledge and skills to complete the money map together. You can also complete the map individually and then share your insights with each other. Real financial power taps into the ever-present possibilities that are always available to you, and the money map is a tool you can use repeatedly to assess where you are and where you are growing and going.

Chapter Three Review

Questions for Reflection

1) How do I feel about completing the money map? What do I need to move forward: an inner decision, outside help, etc.?

2) Where are my areas of strength and my areas for development as I look at the money map? How do I feel about the quality of my spirituality, the content of my beliefs, and the nature of the habits in my money life?

Ideas for Action

1) Complete a more visually dramatic and detailed money map.

2) Share your map and insights about what's so and what's possible with a supportive friend or prosperity partner. Ask for feedback, encouragement or challenges that would best serve your growth.

Tools

Visit **www.themoneykeys.com/tools** to listen to the audio guide *Your Money Map* and download *The Money Map* sample.

Chapter Four

Spirituality: Finding Permanent Peace of Mind

"You will never be financially secure
until you are spiritually secure."

– Sharon Riddell

Chapter Four

Barbara and Tom sat with Ralph, their long time CPA. Ralph was a fast worker, sharp, technologically savvy and up on all the latest tax laws that affected his mostly middle class, professional, family clientele. He'd done a great job of preparing income tax returns for Barbara and Tom, which had been complicated in the past few years, with the arrival of a new baby and a job change for Tom. However, this meeting was a turning point.

Barbara and Tom had made a commitment to expand themselves and their wealth by investing in real estate and by viewing a DVD about the *Law of Attraction*. Newly aware of how much a person's spiritual, mental and emotional energy influences his or her use of money, Barbara and Tom were surprised by Ralph's tone and the content and feeling behind their conversation with him. Every strategy he suggested was a tactic based on preventing bad things from happening: worries about audits, concerns over mistakes, possible changes in the economy, anxieties about losing ground, etc.

They shared with Ralph their excitement about purchasing their first real estate investment property. Ralph looked down, sighed and shook his head back and forth. "I'm just too afraid," he said and launched into a detailed warning about the perils of real estate investing.

Barbara and Tom realized that they needed to deepen their own faith in the larger reality of life. As they grew in financial sophistication, they needed to be aware of the worldview and beliefs of those with whom they interact regarding how they accumulate and use money.

Ralph, the CPA, probably has access to good information for his clients about trends in the market and the tax consequences of real estate investing. But he's caught in the money trap of scarcity. His attention serves fear, anxiety and worry. He's not fully present and available to his clients, and his spiritual source, his wisdom and his power are not fully available to him.

A Sense of Separation

Ralph's reactions are not unusual. Anxiety about money pervades our Western culture. As much as our media and cultural attention focus on glamour, riches and winning prizes, we also have a constant, nervous conversation about losing, making mistakes, getting cheated and suffering financial disasters. We worry that there are not enough time, resources, deals, education, opportunity, land, businesses, clients, people, energy or information. Spiritual scarcity within our minds and hearts manifests into our finances as debt, bankruptcy, fatigue, chaos, hoarding and over-spending.

Anxiety and worry are different from fear. This is an important distinction to emphasize. Fear in the human body is a natural instinct for human survival. Gavin DeBecker wrote a wonderful book called *The Gift of Fear,* in which he identified the fact that the physical sense of fear is our intuitive sense that there is a threat to us in the environment. He showed repeatedly that in situations of physical security and safety, an individual's instincts and intuition are often correct.

The emotional energy most people experience concerning money is not really fear. You may be preoccupied about bills to pay or your children's education, or you may be unsure about where your business is heading. It's unlikely that at this very moment you are actually experiencing a physical threat to your money or well-being. But if you are imagining yourself out on the streets or unable to feed your family, you are creating a sensation in the mind and body that feels like a threat.

The basic anxiety about money comes from an idea, a thought and a sense of separation. You think you're a finite being defined by your income statement and your balance sheet. If you feel you are not a part of the eternal, abundant, infinite source of the all-good, then you get scared. The problem of scarcity is an issue of faith, and the solution is a spiritual connection to your wholeness.

Peace of Mind Is Not a Dollar Amount

What do people really want to do with their money? In all the research, interviews and workshops I completed as research for this book, the number one thing that people said they really want is not millions of dollars, but *peace of mind.*

Financial peace, freedom and power do not come from a dollar amount, even a "big" dollar amount. The symbols, the amounts, the dollars are neutral. There is no net worth that will take away worry. No digit, number or sum exists that provides a permanent sense of freedom and well-being.

Real financial freedom is the spiritual realization of wholeness that gets expressed through thoughts, feelings, beliefs, actions and numbers. True prosperity comes from a state of mind and spirit, and it is a sense of being at one with the truth, the whole, the fullness, the abundance, the flow, the grace and the power of life.

You don't want to be anxious about money. You want to give up worry and distraction. Peace is your ultimate goal.

What Traps You?

Just as each individual has unique qualities, everyone has individualized anxieties and worries around money. Worry about money is an internal state of heart, mind and spirit. Feelings of lack, worry and separation concerning money can be either intense or subtle.

Being self-aware is powerful. When you know yourself well enough to identify the thoughts, conditions, situations and reactions that trigger you into anxiety, you establish a foundation for building the faith you need. Using the categories below, pinpoint the anxieties to which you're most susceptible. When you know what traps you, you can more deliberately choose spiritual qualities and practices that make sense for you. Which of the following describe your present financial worries?

- I'm alone.
- I've got to figure out how to make this happen.
- I've made mistakes about money, and it's tough to come back.
- I don't know what I'm doing in this area; it's hard for people.
- Money comes between people.
- You can't make money in art, music, healing, etc.
- There's not enough.
- Someone else has all the money and education, resources and advantages.
- The rich are greedy, and that's just the way it is.
- The good opportunities are gone.
- We've trashed the planet, and we're in trouble.
- The market is changing; I should've gotten in (or out) last year.

- Time's running out.

- It's not for me.

- People like me can't get ahead.

- My boss, parents or ex have hurt my chances.

- I never learned how to make money.

- Focusing on money will take me away from my family or God.

- I've cheated or failed with money, and it's over for me.

Worries Require a Backup Plan

We all have backup plans in our financial lives. It's the strategies we will use if our worries turn out to be true. We have a backup plan if our lover or partner gets sick or leaves. A backup plan if we get sick. A backup plan if our parents, children, or other family members are gone. A backup plan if the job, the business, the market or the government goes awry.

Most people have thought about the "what ifs" somewhere along the line. What would you do? Where would you go? How would you survive? The backup plan may have been articulated, or it may never have been spoken. Backup plans based on worries have a different spiritual, mental and emotional energy than deliberate decisions about legal structuring, insurance policies and practical contingency plans. They're quiet, lurking doubts turned into strategies for coping.

For me, the underlying backup was, "Well, I could always work hard" because I know I can work hard. I have proven my work ethic for forty years, and I believe in hard work. My backup plan was, "I can have what I want if I am willing to work hard and struggle." No wonder I felt so deeply guided to develop my spirituality. I was tired! In the midst of a workshop, with tears running down my face, I felt literally exhausted. I could not continue living under the influence of the idea that money comes from hard work and struggle. Discovering and articulating my backup plan showed me that my anxiety trap was the idea that I'm not worthy unless I'm producing. On my desert island, I was a hamster on the wheel with no way off. I needed a better reality to serve with my time, energy and attention. I needed a divine backup plan.

What Reality Are You Serving?

If you choose to place your energy, attention and resources into cultivating a relationship with your creative source, you are serving a reality of wholeness. This reality is based on the premise that you are already at one with the infinite, eternal, loving source of life itself. You are more than your physical body, personal history and possessions. You are a spiritual being with an essence that never dies. You are permanently at one with a friendly and ever-expanding universe.

The Law of Unity

The *Law of Unity* is the universal principle of building a spirituality of wholeness. The *Law of Unity* states that all of life is connected to and created from one infinite, eternal source. This source is also known as God, Creator, Life, Spirit, the Universe, Higher Power, Mother Earth, and more. The nature of the source is intelligence, power, love, invisibility, creativity, wholeness, peace, freedom, joy and abundance. Being the source of all, its nature is inherent in all of creation, including humanity. We are one with life. Everything and everyone is interconnected, not the same, but connected. When we live from our awareness of the reality of *Law of Unity*, we serve wholeness.

Scarcity Thrives on Duality

When you deepen your faith in the *Law of Unity*, you may notice all the ways people consciously or unconsciously operate from a sense of duality. The duality mindset divides things into good and bad and keeps you fearful.

A good analogy is food and diets. In many diets over the years, the main idea has been to make something wrong, and thus something to avoid, like a certain kind of carbohydrate or "bad" fat. Suddenly bananas and carrots are "out" and berries and green beans are "in."

There can be similar themes in some money management techniques. Lattés, new cars, mutual funds, paying off your consumer debt or being someone's employee are all neutral things. They are bad if we believe they are bad.

Is it possible to be wealthy and still enjoy a daily latté? Is it possible to create wealth and still drive a new car? Can mutual funds be part of a successful portfolio? What's the role of being an employee versus being your own boss? Are IRS agents really doing the work of the "dark side?" Is insurance a racket or a necessity?

With faith in the *Law of Unity*, you can identify when the reality behind a certain bit of advice or a financial strategy is emphasizing scarcity, superstition or lack.

The Reality of Wholeness

The creative source of life is all love, all energy, all information, all power and all good. Creation is a reflection of this source, created in its own image and likeness. This reality is an infinite presence, with which many feel a personal relationship and connection as their own "God."

This presence is transcendent, above and beyond our human experiences, personalities and history. This presence is within us, expressed through our thoughts, soul and consciousness. As individual beings, we are expressions of our creative source, whatever we believe that to be.

The philosophy of Religious Science is, "All that I am is God, but I am not all that God is." We are the divine expressing itself through our individuality. Wholeness is the state of spiritual sufficiency, meaning that everything we need is provided for. Who we are is an intelligent, creative, perfect being.

The *Law of Unity* tells us that wholeness is our spiritual nature. Even in the midst of human imperfection and experiences of lack, our wholeness is present. Wholeness is not defined by or dependent on any fact or condition that comes and goes, like net worth or physical bodies. Wholeness is a state of being.

Religion, Unity and Wholeness

Throughout spiritual history there is a thread of beliefs, practices and feelings called mysticism. The term comes from the Greek (*mustikos*) meaning "an initiate." Mysticism is the pursuit of achieving communion with ultimate reality, the divine,s piritual truth through direct revelation, intuition or insight. What is powerful to note is that the major world religions of Christianity, Judaism, Islam, Buddhism and Hinduism, as well as contemporary spiritual systems such as New Thought or the Baha'i practices, have a mystical sect, group of practices, and teachings.

The essence of the mystical message is that life is essentially a unified whole, that we are one with a larger reality beyond our physical perceptions and experiences, and that the nature of God/Source/Life is loving goodness. To develop peace of mind about your financial life through spirituality, you can have a religious view or not.

The Buddhists teach that the nature of the Buddha, the state of enlightenment, is available to all. Our human suffering comes from attachment to the ideas, things and symbols of this world, which come and go. Enlightenment is the state of releasing those attachments. Dominic J. Houlder and Kulananda Houlder, authors of *Mindfulness and Money: The Buddhist Path to Abundance*, claim that a mindful practice and a conscious financial life are not incompatible, "No money, no civilization. No civilization, no spirituality. Few of us could be concerned with Enlightenment in a world of brutish enslavement to mere survival."

The sacred texts of Hinduism, the *Vedas*, tell us that "thou art that." Each one of us has within us the ineffable, un-manifest, great reality of life. The supreme absolute presence of the divine, revealed through many gods and goddesses, is also awake in us all. The Hindu goddess Lakshmi represents the prosperous, abundant nature of life, and she is widely celebrated.

Mystical Christianity points to the Kingdom of God being within us. When Jesus stated, "I and my Father are one," he proclaimed a mystical union. Loaves and fishes are multiplied and the thousands are fed when we look to ever-present spiritual supply as our creative source. Many of the classic prosperity teachers of the 19th and 20th centuries, such as Catherine Ponder and Emmet Fox, use the miracle stories, the parables and the teachings of Jesus as examples of serving a reality of wholeness.

In Judaism, in the mystical teaching of the *Kabala*, the true essence of the divine is so transcendent that it cannot be described, except with reference to what it is not. "Ein Sof," which literally means "without end," encompasses the idea of the omnipresence of divinity. To practice these teachings is to surrender and release the concerns and negativity of the human ego and to cultivate the affinity and connection with the essence of the divine.

Sufism is the mystical aspect of Islam, where self-realization and God-realization dance together. The Sufi master encourages us to "keep your hands busy with your duties in this world while your heart is busy with God." The work of the Sufi poet Rumi shows the mystical love affair with the divine.

Indeed, an open view of religious traditions supports the *Law of Unity*, the reality of wholeness, and the possibility of peace of mind in every aspect of living, including our money.

The great spiritual leaders and figures of the ages are often referred to as mystics, based on their direct perception of life as a unified whole that transcends logic, fact or physical evidence. The suggestion here is that we all have the mystical capacity within us because we are at one with the source of life. Releasing your anxieties and ideas of separation and foregoing your attachment to physical symbols such as money are ways that you cultivate your mystical nature. Your primary identity as a spiritual being is your birthright of unity with your source, which is whole, sufficient, plentiful, intelligent, powerful and loving.

If you believe yourself to be separate from life, then you will experience life as separate, apart, different. You suffer when you feel a sense of separation from your truth. You are released from suffering when you realize a sense of unity. If you believe yourself to be at one with a friendly universe, at one with the source of all creation, then you, by your nature, reproduce, reflect and express that infinite reality.

91

Developing the Divine Backup Plan

Soothing your worries about money doesn't come from having more dollars; it comes from realizing and living from an awareness of your spiritual nature. The questions, "Is there enough?" "Am I worthy?" "Am I free?" "Will I die?" are the existential questions which are underneath the anxieties and worries of a belief in scarcity. To answer these questions, you develop a personal relationship with the higher power of your understanding, cultivate your communion with spiritual qualities, strengthen your inner faith, and then think, feel and act in your financial affairs.

For me to get off the desert island, I created a divine backup plan based on the premise that God is my source. Period. That's the foundation of faith on which I lean. My peace of mind does not depend on my body being strong, my intellect sharp, my efforts productive or my investments profitable. My ultimate freedom and security come from my profound belief that I am at one with a friendly universe, and the presence of God deep within me and all around me is my one source of supply. *Living* the divine plan is a consistent practice for me of developing my spirituality.

Now it's your turn to discover and cultivate the spirituality that's right for you.

- "I'm alone" becomes "My source is everywhere present." You'll want to develop your feeling of the omnipresence of the divine in your spirituality.

- "There's not enough" invites "The supply is infinite." You'll study and affirm and know that the affluence, infinite intelligence and abundant nature of the divine are always available.

- "It's not for me" is a call for feeling oneness. It invites "I am connected to the universal source." Your great comfort is remembering that you are made purposefully in the image and likeness of your creative source.

Cultivating Your Spiritual Qualities

We are one with all of life, but we're not all the same. Each of us is a unique expression of the divine. It's powerful to find the particular ways the infinite reveals as you. Knowing what you desire and why you desire it helps you create the specific spiritual qualities to cultivate in your spirituality.

Spiritual qualities are invisible, creative attributes of the divine. Love, peace, joy, freedom, beauty, order, wholeness, abundance, truth and wisdom are all qualities that are unconditional. They don't begin and end with the changeable nature of human life. Cheerfulness is a human emotion; joy is a spiritual quality. When you cultivate a spiritual quality, you build your relationship to it. There's always more to discover about the nature of peace, freedom or wisdom.

What inspires, motivates and drives you? *Why* are you pursuing the spiritual experience? *Why* are you looking to build your wealth? The genuine answer to those questions is your "why." Your "why" is a more important motivation for expression than what you say you want or what others think.

If a counseling client says, "I want a lover, a healthy body, a million dollars, a hit record, peace on earth and a new car," a smart spiritual counselor asks, "Why?" If you had all of that, then what? What would you feel? What would you think? What would you get? Who would you be? The answers to those questions usually point to an intangible, spiritual quality.

Romancing the Spirit

Once you have a sense of the spiritual qualities you seek to empower, it takes time, energy and passion to deepen your realization of spiritual truth. One of my great teachers, Rev. Nirvana Gayle, used to describe this as "romancing the spirit." Having a vibrant spiritual practice is much like meeting a new lover. There is a certain kind of energy that fills you so that you do whatever it takes to be with your beloved.

When I first met my partner Bill, I lived in Los Angeles and he lived in Phoenix, Arizona. It seemed easy to hop in the car and drive 362 miles to be with my beloved. If I could be there for an evening, it was worth it. The laundry could wait. I was inspired and committed and willing to hop in the car. That kind of passion, interest and connection is also possible when you desire to have a deeper communion with the divine.

Spirituality for Permanent Peace of Mind

The dynamic of being lost and then found is one of the profound archetypes of spiritual realization. We fall asleep to the truth, and we awaken into it. We forget, and then we remember. We feel separation, and then we reconnect.

Developing your spirituality through study, contemplation, celebration and application of principles and practices is how you reconnect. You don't have to *try* to be spiritual; your nature *is* spiritual. You don't have to *become* more spiritual; you're already infinite spirit. You don't have to *bring* spirituality into your investments, workplace or finances; spirituality is already there.

Spiritual practice doesn't have to be difficult or complicated. It's often as simple as relaxing and letting go. Then, all you ever need to do is notice when you forget the truth (you feel scared) and decide in that moment to remember. That's what spiritual practice is.

Today's entertainment media often depict someone who is "spiritual" as a caricature, such as an intolerant, religious fundamentalist, a pious saint, or a New Age nut. Using this book, you're creating a different model of living a spiritual life. You can have both success in worldly results and a deep faith and communion with spiritual truths. Peace of mind is worth finding your way to incorporate a deeper realization of the *Law of Unity* and the reality of wholeness for yourself.

Practices for Developing Your Spirituality

The practices to deepen your spiritual realization are gratitude, meditation, inspiration, and visioning. These are practices everyone can incorporate into regular practice in the methods and modes that work best for your personality, lifestyle and interests.

Gratitude Enhances Everything

Gratitude is one of the most powerful spiritual practices to use in living a wealthy life. The nature of divine reality is giving. When you are grateful, you emulate your divine creative source. Being thankful is also one of the easiest practices to incorporate into a busy life. Give thanks for what is already around you and, through your appreciation, prepare yourself to receive more.

There are simple ways to apply gratitude to money and its meaning in your life.

- Food and nourishment symbolize the gifts of the divine, and many people include saying "thanks" as a blessing before meals.

- You can explicitly and verbally give thanks to your creative source as you deposit your paycheck, see your investment returns or book new business with clients.

- Keeping a gratitude journal is a beautiful practice. Every day, write a list of things for which you are grateful. Some people like to keep a journal by their bedside and write in it immediately upon awakening, in order to begin the day in gratitude. Others find it comforting and sacred to write their list at day's end. The objects of your gratitude can be people, ideas, experiences, things, memories, anything. Start with two or three items per day. Once you start, you'll see how easy it is to find more to be grateful for. See if you can work up to giving thanks for twenty-five items per day.

Another practice is "Guerilla Gratitude," a process for finding thankfulness whether you feel like it or not! Sometimes when you're afraid, resentful, exhausted, or otherwise feeling separate, gratitude seems inauthentic or hard to find. Those are great times for starting from where you are and working yourself into an authentic sense of thankfulness and connection. Following is a worksheet to guide you through your own "Guerilla Gratitude."

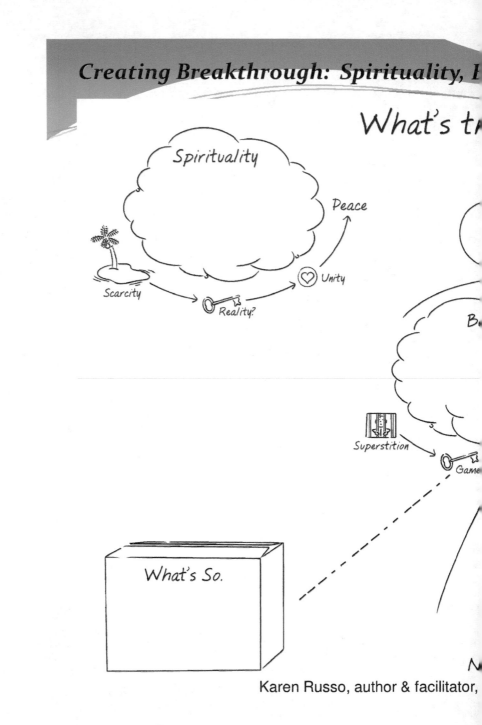

Karen Russo, author & facilitator,

Money For?

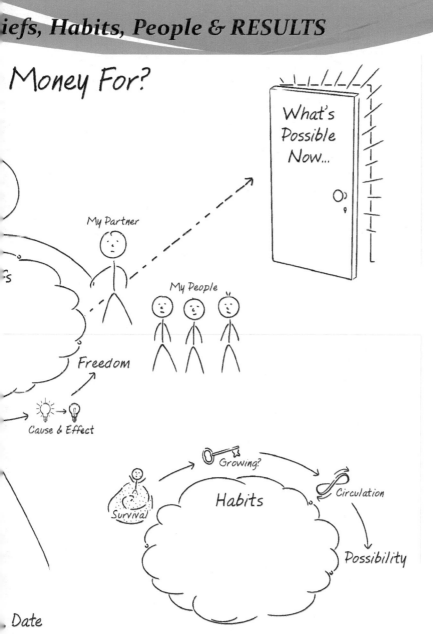

What's Possible Now...

My Partner

My People

Freedom

Cause & Effect

Growing?

Survival

Habits

Circulation

Possibility

Date

.TheMoneyKeys.com, 877 249 0194

The Money Keys Practice: Guerilla Gratitude

Center:

- Bring yourself into the present moment with three deep breaths, in through the nose and out through the nose and mouth.

What's not:

- Look around you and notice all the "bad" things that aren't happening to you or your family.

- Make a mental or written list of three items: "I'm grateful that I'm not (in bankruptcy, on the streets, back ten years ago, struggling like _____)."

What's so:

- Look around you and notice all the resources, support and supply you have.

- Make a mental or written list of three items: "I'm grateful for (the money we have, the work I do, the home I'm in, the opportunities I've been given)."

What's real:

- Close your eyes and put your attention on your inner spiritual insights, thoughts, emotions and energy.

- Make a mental or written list of three items: "I'm grateful for (wisdom, spiritual truth, beauty of art, feelings of freedom when I let go of the past, love for family and power of prayer)."

Say thank you:

- Turn to your divine, creative source and give thanks.

Meditation: Emptying the Cup

The wise monk received a pompous young scholar who wanted to be taught the path to enlightenment. The monk served his earnest guest some tea. He poured his visitor's cup full and then kept on pouring. The young student watched the overflow until he could restrain himself no longer. "It is overfull. No more will go in!" "Like this cup," the monk said, "You are full of your own opinions and ideas. How can I show you anything unless you first empty your cup?"

Like the teacup, meditation is one of the ancient practices of communing with the divine, of emptying the self of the thoughts, sensations and concerns of the physical self, the personality and the ego. The purpose of meditation is to commune with your own inner, spiritual nature. There are many paths, practices and modes of meditation. For the purpose of releasing anxiety about money, I emphasize the capacity of meditation to still the churning of the surface mind in order to access peacefulness.

Meditation dedicated to stillness helps you tap into the gaps between the mental content of thoughts. In meditation, you notice the nothingness out of which everything emerges, and by doing so, you clear away the surface conversation and the chatter of the material world. You consciously commune with inner stillness that helps you detach from identifying yourself solely as a body, a personality, the roles you play and the possessions you have.

Meditation can be much more restorative than just zoning out. Watching your favorite television show, working Sudoku puzzles, or surfing the Internet allows you to relax, but that's not meditation.

Developing a meditation practice to enhance your peace of mind around money (and everything else) requires that you attend to the stillness that emerges out of the void, the gap between the thoughts. You can use a mantra, a repeated sound or phrase, to focus your attention. Then when the mind wanders, you gently use your mantra to return your attention to the stillness. Observing the rhythmic nature of the breath is another way to clear out the chatter of daily living and allow the deep restorative nature of stillness to reveal peace to you.

The best way to begin meditation is to just start. Choose a regular time, place and process for meditation that fits your schedule and preferences. Many find that meditating for fifteen to twenty minutes in the morning and in the evening provides a great basis for overall balance and well-being. But even if you dedicate five minutes of silence in the mornings to attending to your breath and feeling the presence of stillness before conversation, email, television and commuting, you will find something changes in your life.

Be willing to learn, practice and grow. If you are serious about experiencing permanent peace of mind about money (or anything else), you deserve to invest time, energy and resources in cultivating peace. Having a regular meditation practice is powerful. *The Money Keys* practice provided on the next page is a simple practice for peace of mind.

The Money Keys Practice: Peace Be Still Meditation

Prepare:

- Turn away from external distractions.
- Find a comfortable, quiet place to sit.
- Close your eyes and breathe naturally for a minute or so.

Center:

- Take three deep breaths, in through the nose and out through the nose and mouth.
- Consciously dedicate your meditation to serving your higher power and the reality of wholeness.
- You can say "I surrender" out loud.

Peace, be still:

- As you sit and breathe, relaxed and calm, thoughts and sensations may arise. Resist nothing.
- When thoughts come, simply say to yourself, "Peace, be still."
- Notice the thoughts also change and go.
- You don't need to try to think or not think. Just be, breathe and say to yourself, as needed, "Peace, be still."
- Continue for fifteen to twenty minutes.

> *Blessing:*
> - With no judgment or evaluation, allow the meditation to conclude.
> - Say something like, "I give thanks for everything, the thoughts, the stillness, everything. I bless myself. I go in peace."

Inspiration

Meditation helps you empty yourself of the mind chatter and distractions where scarcity tends to thrive. When you are peaceful, balanced and clear, you can fill yourself with inspirational practices. You cultivate a deeper knowledge of and a feeling for spiritual principles like the *Law of Unity* and spiritual qualities like wholeness, love, grace, power, truth, freedom, joy and beauty. These practices fill us up.

Infuse your mind, your heart, your body and your awareness with spiritual images, messages and content. Following are a few ideas:

- Read books, listen to CDs and watch programs with spiritual teachings and topics.
- Involve the physical senses with nature, dancing, yoga, music and chanting.
- Contemplate sacred literature or poetry.
- Share, create or enjoy inspired art.

Spiritual ideas must be "caught" or discerned spiritually. It's not just about getting information about the divine; it's about feeling a personal connection with the divine. When you feel yourself at one with your source, you are at peace. If you fill your mind, time and energy with violent news, harsh images and dramatic stories of unhappy people and victims of the world, you add that vibration and information to your energy field. Inspiration requires purposefully turning toward the people, images and ideas that connect you to your heart, your soul, your wholeness.

Start where you are. What inspires you? What makes you feel peaceful and connected to your source? Inspirational practices are consciously *adding* the positive energy and information that uplifts you the most. Following is a simple inspirational practice for feeling your connection to wholeness.

The Money Keys Practice:
"You Belong to the Universe" Inspiration

Prepare:
- Set aside ten to fifteen minutes.
- Create an inspiring, undistracted environment.

Center:
- Take three deep breaths, in through the nose and out through the nose and mouth.
- Consciously open this inspiration to feeling your connection with the divine. You can say, "I surrender" out loud.

Chant:

- Listen to and chant along with a spiritually uplifting song or chant such as "Be Still" by Orgena Rose, "I am So Blessed" by Karen Drucker, or "All that I Am" by Daniel Nahmod.

The Word:

- Read aloud an inspiring passage, in first person, such as the following from Dr. Ernest Holmes' *This Thing Called You*:

I belong to the universe in which I live. I am one with Creative Genius back of this vast array of ceaseless motion, this original flow of life. I am as much a part of it as the sun, the earth and the air. There is something in me telling me this—like a voice echoing from some mountaintop of inward vision, like a light whose origin no one has seen, like an impulse welling up from an invisible source. My soul belongs to the universe. I sense my oneness with all life. I enter into the joy of conscious union with Infinite Peace, Divine Joy and Complete Security.

Open:

- Be still for a few minutes and feel the images, insights and sensations that arise in you.

Blessing:

- Gently allow the period of inspiration to conclude. Say something like, "I give thanks for the divine, I bless myself and all of life. All is well."

You may find that starting your day with inspiration and concluding it with meditation works for you, or the other way around. The two practices go hand in hand for creating a deeper spiritual communion.

Visioning

The visioning practice has been a part of my life for over ten years. I was first introduced to it at the Agape Spiritual Center in Los Angeles by Dr. Michael Beckwith.

Visioning strengthens your spiritual intuition as you access inspiring ideas about who you are and where you're going. It can also create new possibilities for money and what it means to you. For your peace of mind about money to be independent of your financial circumstances, you need to depend upon a connection to a greater power that extends beyond your financial life. Visioning is a powerful spiritual practice for connecting to the unknown, yet-to-be-imagined aspects of the divine. Visioning is spiritually uplifting because you "catch" something greater or beyond the best of your past experiences. You can also access ideas and inspirations that are beyond the realm of the ego.

In visioning, you enter into a meditative and receptive state. You become quiet and still. You open yourself to the unconditional realm of inspiration and consciousness where ideas, information and insights are always flowing. You are open to thinking the thoughts of God.

With your attention and energy focused on your highest feeling of oneness with the divine, you ask yourself (or the individual leading the visioning asks you) a series of questions. The questions usually follow a process, going from broad to specific, from spiritual to practical. You listen within and see what emerges as answers. The answers do not flow from a being up in the sky, separate from you; rather, you connect to the divine mind within you, the higher self of your own being.

Questions include the following:

1) *What is the high spiritual vision of my wealth, this project, my business, my job or this relationship?*

   This vision question often elicits vivid symbols or imagery, abstract ideas, or lofty purpose and direction.

2) *What must I be in consciousness to serve the vision?*

   What emerges from this question are things that can be expressed as spiritual qualities, such as love, peace, freedom, joy, abundance, order, power, truth and wholeness. These ideas are timeless and unconditional, creative qualities you can always aspire to increase and reveal in your life.

3) *What, if anything, is to be released?*

   This question helps to reveal what to stop or release. It could be habits, beliefs, energy, relationships or even practical issues. Much of spiritual growth is simply letting go of that which no longer serves you. When it comes to a money life, many people hold onto thoughts and feelings that are not in alignment with the truth of who they really are. In the visioning practice, you can quickly identify those beliefs that block the full expression of your vision.

4) *What, if anything, is to be embraced?*

Quantum scientists tell us that everything is energy and energy cannot be destroyed, only transformed. If you are releasing the things that don't serve you, then you have the opportunity to consciously choose and strengthen the things you do desire. The answer to this visioning question is often to add particular spiritual practices or to deepen your faith in qualities or beliefs toward which you are moving.

5) *Anything Else?*

This question opens you to any other insights or inspirations, information or images available to you. For those who are open to intuitive guidance, this question allows for both the expected and the unexpected to emerge.

Answers come in a variety of ways: images, feelings, ideas, information, words, sensations, etc. It is also common to feel like nothing is happening in visioning. Over time, inspirations and insights emerge in a variety of ways. The content from visioning practice is often the elements behind the doorway leading into "What's Possible" on your money map.

Visioning in a group is enlivening. Spirit speaks through all of us. The one mind of God is at work with synchronicity. Maybe everyone in the group catches something similar, like the quality of joy when introducing a new product, or the idea of circulation in a new venture, or even the color red that relates to passion in a relationship.

Below is a simple process for getting started with visioning on your own or with a partner or group.

The Money Keys Practice: My Wealth Vision

Prepare:

- Set aside twenty to thirty minutes.
- Create an inspiring, undistracted environment.

Center:

- Take three deep breaths, in through the nose and out through the nose and mouth.
- Consciously open to your connection with the divine.
- You can say "I surrender" out loud.

Opening blessing:

- Begin with a blessing, such as:

How good it is to feel the presence of the divine. I open myself to the infinite reality that is the creative source of all of life. Spirit is. I am. We are. Life is. I am at one with the wholeness, intelligence, grace, power, truth, abundance, flow and beauty of life itself. The invisible, creative, eternal vibration of life is flowing through me. I welcome inspiration, insight and wisdom to pour forward through me in the wealth vision of my life.

Questions and stillness:

- For each of the following questions, pose the question out loud and sit in stillness for three to five minutes.

- Capture the insights, images or ideas that emerge in your journal.

- What is the high spiritual vision of a wealthy life for me?

- Who must I be in consciousness to serve this vision of a wealth life?

- What, if anything, must I release?

- What, if anything, must I embrace?

- Anything else?

- Allow the themes and messages from the vision to become part of your money map, your spiritual practices and the development of your beliefs and habits.

Blessing:

- Gently allow the visioning to conclude.

- Say something like, "I give thanks for the divine inspiration and vision that is always revealing itself as me, as wealth, as all. I bless myself and all of life. All is well."

What does it look and feel like when you cultivate a comprehensive spirituality that includes practices like gratitude, meditation, inspiration and visioning? Everyone has his or her own journey. Gary's story is a good example of allowing spiritual truths to bring us into new ideas of who we are and what is possible.

Gary's Story

My family is from Appalachia. We weren't poor, but my parents had to work hard to keep my sister and me fed and to pay for the $12,000 house we were raised in. Money was always tight.

My parents married when my father was seventeen and my mother just fifteen. They met in a small, one-room country church when he was eleven and she was nine. He used to ride his bike to see her.

After they got married, they lived in the back of my grandfather's garage on the farm. My father did odd jobs to get by.

"Eight hours work for eight hours pay." "It's supposed to be work; that's why it's called that." "Get it before someone else gets it." "Hoard money because something could go wrong." These are the things I heard about money as a child. Why replace something when it's working, even though the sweeper is thirty years old and weighs a ton or the hand mixer has only one working beater?

My family believed in God and heaven and being good, but there wasn't a sense that God had much to do with paying the bills or our little problems.

I took those ideas into my adult life. Anything I've ever done has been self-taught and hard work. I've been a disc jockey, songwriter, writer, guitarist, artist, entertainment booking agent, PR Director, and so on. I've worked hard but continued to only have enough money to get by.

What used to get me was not having enough to pay a bill. If I had $1,000 in bills and had a generous portion left over, I'd be fine. But if I was at the point where I couldn't pay a bill for weeks until I got paid again, with little or no spending money, then I'd have gotten angry and depressed.

As I grew, I wanted freedom from the energy-sucking thoughts that I had to work for someone else to have something. I wanted freedom to choose my hours and freedom to make my own decisions. I came to a spiritual teaching because I knew I needed to shift my perspective to find freedom and connection, regardless of the amount of money I was making.

Through the classes, I began to study principles like oneness and the Law of Cause and Effect and saw how these metaphysical ideas showed up in my life. I started to meditate, to clear my mind and to create a sense of who I am from the inside. I developed a connection with Spirit as love and with the interconnectedness of all of life. I learned about the Law of Circulation and started to purposely see money as a flow.

My attitudes about money have changed. I've always thought that I never desired a ton of money, though I'm now open to it.

I think one of the biggest things I've learned recently was grasping the value of something versus its cost. I was stuck in this pattern of always looking at the cost of an item or service. I estimated something's value by figuring out how much I had to shell out?

I was mulling over buying two plane tickets to go back home for the holidays. I cringed when I saw the prices one Saturday night as I scanned websites for flights. Because of demand, prices were much higher around holidays. To prove to myself the greed of airlines, I looked at the same flights two weeks into January. The fares were around one third of the price I was looking at paying. I shut the computer off.

That Monday I was in a session with my spiritual counselor, focusing on abundance, money and prosperity. She helped me see the value versus the cost. It didn't hit me until the next night. Pow! The debate about whether I was flying my girlfriend and me back home was over. I realized that the value of having her along with me and sharing my past with her was immeasurable. It's an inner value that's priceless to me. Its value was more than I was being asked to pay. The minute I got home that night, I called the airlines and secured two flights and put a rental car on hold.

I try to bring this value versus cost thinking to all I do now. If I see something I would like to buy, I scan the value versus the cost. One outweighs the other every time. For example, there is a funky pair of urban cowboy boots I would love to have, but they cost $475. Instead of feeling like I don't have the money to pay for them, which I actually do, or getting upset that I can't buy this or that, I merely do the value/cost comparison. I still see them on the shelf. I say to myself that they cost more than the value they have for me. Perhaps if they went on sale at half-off I'd reconsider.

It's a completely different mindset. It's empowering. No longer can people dictate "their" price, and require that I pay it or get depressed. Now I'm in the driver's seat doing the choosing.

I've also been through the visioning process and can see that sharing value is a strong idea for me as an artist and a professional. I'm not just a writer; I share the value of ideas and information. I don't just work; I bring value. I'm not just paid for my time or output; I circulate value. All of the spiritual truths I've learned and practiced have helped me change my perspective. I feel more connected to life, more optimistic, and free about money that I ever dreamed possible.

Divine Mysteries

If we are already complete, whole, and at one with our creative source, why do we develop a spiritual practice? The paradox is that while we are already whole, it is the nature of the divine to ever expand. There's always more of the infinite, and more of us, to be revealed. Spiritual growth is both incremental and transformative. The spiritual practices of gratitude, meditation, inspiration and visioning help you develop a greater sense of peace about the nature of life that grows slowly in a linear way. Your daily meditation gets incrementally longer by a few minutes each week, and you build upon that growth over time. Spiritual growth can also be transformative, like a bolt of lightening out of the blue. For example, you could be writing in your gratitude journal and suddenly have a dramatic reorientation to who you are, what life is about, and what it all means. It would have a profound effect.

When you are more spiritually self-aware, you are also better able to stop being self-obsessed. As you deepen your spirituality, you will identify financial worries as just thoughts of separation and not the truth of your being. When you're more peaceful and more present, you'll be more available and effective in every aspect of your life.

Chapter Four Review

Questions for Reflection

1) What have been the money traps that have led to my money worries? What has been my backup plan?

2) How does my religious background (or lack of one) contribute to my spirituality and relationship with my creative source?

3) What do I notice about duality and separation in my thoughts, feelings and actions around money? How do I relate to the *Law of Unity*?

4) What are the specific qualities I most want to cultivate in my spirituality? What attributes of wholeness, such as grace, love, peace, freedom, wisdom, power, truth, beauty, order, right action, abundance and joy most inspire and resonate with me?

Ideas for Action

1) Take a wealth and spirituality retreat.

- By yourself or with a prosperity partner, mate or friend, set aside several hours or several days to deepen your spiritual life concerning money and its meaning.

- Turn off the technology and the distractions.

- If you can, go to a retreat center or quiet environment in nature.

- Use the practices of gratitude, meditation, inspiration and visioning.

- Find what processes work best for you and commit to a regular practice you can incorporate into your daily life.

Tools

E-mail **prayer@themoneykeys.com** for *A Prayer for You*. Provide us with your name, e-mail address and phone number along with your prayer request, including the phrases you choose for your higher power, the spiritual qualities you're cultivating and the vision you have around money and its meaning. We will record a prayer just for you that you can use in your spiritual practice.

Chapter Five

Beliefs: Choosing Freedom in the Money Game

"Nothing is true but thinking makes it so."

– William Shakespeare

Chapter Five

When Jack was nine years old, his favorite uncle surprised him with a handful of quarters "just for fun." Jack knew his mother would make him share the money with his younger sister. So he spent as much as he could on candy and toys at the local dime store, then he felt bad when his mother scolded him for being selfish. His mother made him give the remainder of the coins to his sister.

Forty years later, in a workshop on wealth consciousness, Jack did an exercise where he inventoried the emotionally intense, memorable money moments in his life and looked for how early experiences were repeated later in life. He shook his head and smiled. He could see the pattern. When extra money came in, he'd spend it quickly, afraid that if he didn't it could be taken away. Although Jack had forty years of fun with sporting gear, cars, trucks and motorcycles, he hadn't amassed assets that could produce income in the future. He's been divorced twice, both times allowing guilt to ravage his assets. Jack's inventory helped him identify his beliefs. "I can't be trusted with money." "You need to spend it before someone takes it away." "I might not get what I want."

Jack developed a more sophisticated spirituality through studying wealth principles and saw himself as one with the source. In healing these past beliefs, Jack released himself from judgment and also found compassion for his mother in her efforts to teach her children to share.

Jack created new meaning for himself. "I am worthy and valuable." "God is my source, and there's plenty to go around." "I can save and spend money just for me." "Money reflects the integrity and joy of who I am." He established a foundation of new habits. Jack's income grew as he began tithing ten percent of all income, deliberately saving more, and starting a fun account just for himself.

Today, he thinks differently and feels differently about money. He also has more to give, more to share and more to keep.

Choosing new meaning about money is the process of consciously participating with the idea that as you are to life, life is to you. You cooperate with the universal principle, the *Law of Cause and Effect*. You proactively use the practices of inquiry, healing and co-creation. You set the rules, the roles and the goals of a money game you want to play.

Law of Cause and Effect

The *Law of Cause and Effect* is the way creation occurs. For every visible manifestation, there's an invisible idea behind it. Cause refers to invisible, intangible spiritual ideas that are operated upon by the *Law of Cause and Effect* to reveal effects, which are the visible, changeable things and experiences of life. On a universal level, the law reflects back the cause of all creation. On an individual level, our consciousness, the sum total of our thoughts, beliefs and energy is operated upon by the law to produce the effects of our lives. Our experience of life is created through the way we relate to the *Law of Cause and Effect*. The cause is consciousness. Our ideas, attention, awareness, energy and direction, acted upon by the *Law of Cause and Effect*, are revealed as the effects in our lives.

Indeed, these metaphysical laws are automatic. The *Law of Cause and Effect* operates without struggle, effort or strain. The law is also impersonal, which means that it operates for everyone all of the time. The law is operating for each of us whether we know it or not.

More specifically, our individual consciousness co-creates with the one, eternal, infinite consciousness. We are creating, each and every day, whether haphazardly or deliberately. We choose and create at many levels. We choose consciously, subconsciously, individually and collectively. We also choose from the depths of our soul, from the eternal essence of who we are beyond our bodies and historical personalities. We might not be able to logically understand these deeper, soulful "choices" through our conscious minds. While we don't consciously choose bad things, we always choose the meanings we associate with events and, therefore, our experience of life.

The Law as a Mirror, a Magnet and a Magnifier

The Law of Cause and Effect acts in three ways:

1) The *Law* is a mirror, reflecting our past back to us. It shows us what we have believed, intended and done. The results and experiences of our financial lives reflect back to us what we have thought, felt and created in our lives.

2) The *Law* is a magnet here in the present moment. It includes the *Law of Attraction*. What we focus on, we attract to us. Like a magnet, it draws to us that which is like us.

3) The *Law* is a magnifier, a medium through which we magnify ourselves and our beliefs into manifesting the desires we intend for the future. When we consciously want to create new meanings and experiences, the *Law* is the medium through which we co-create those things we want.

The Law Says "Yes"

One of the partner exercises I do in workshops is called "The *Law* Says Yes." Person A speaks about an area of life in which he or she has a desire to create something new. While Person A talks about that area, Person B acts as the *Law*. As the *Law*, Person B is only allowed to say, "The *Law* says yes."

Person A says, "My parents always struggled and fought constantly about money. Money creates stress and conflict. I decided that I would not care so much about money because it would cause conflict for me, too." B says, "The *Law* says yes. The *Law* says yes."

Repeatedly, as A talks about where his or her attention, energies and beliefs have been, particularly with phrases like, "I've always struggled with" or "I don't know how to" or "I really don't want" or "I'm afraid of," B, as the *Law*, says "Yes, yes, yes." After five minutes, the partners switch roles. It doesn't take long for people to feel the power of how they use the *Law*, whether they are consciously aware of it or not.

The *Law* acts upon thoughts, wrapped in emotion, intensified with repetition, enlivened by our words. The *Law* says "Yes." The *Law* is inclusive. The *Law* does not distinguish our interests, our attention, our energy or our speech, as being a "yes" or a "no." We experience what we focus on.

The *Law* is active whether we know it or not, like it or not, or agree with it or not. We can choose to consciously, purposefully and objectively participate with the *Law*, or we can choose to resist it. An abundant, prosperous, wealthy, flowing, satisfying, happy life is one in which we cooperate with the *Law* to reveal the magnificence of who we are.

You will always be disappointed if you look to manipulate the *Law* to manifest things or effects. Effects are symbols of the cause behind them, the spiritual qualities. It's possible to mentally concentrate on symbols and make things happen. But things without meaning come and go and can't provide the peace, freedom and other intangibles that are available.

Choosing New Meaning

Your consciousness, the sum total of your thoughts, feelings, beliefs and energy, creates your perception of the quality of your experiences. Conditions or circumstances, such as mates, jobs, currency, numbers on computer screens and "things out there," do not cause your experience. You perceive and interpret events, choose their meaning, energize thoughts, feel emotional energy and have experiences. Experience is an expression based on perception, which is relative and individualized. Experience is how you interpret life based on your inner spirituality, your ideas and your emotional sensations. This allows you to relate to the circumstances of your life.

There is no one objective, discrete, neutral or factual reality. Everything is perception. One person's rich is another's poor. One person's dream job is another's prison. One person's inspiring outreach program is another's lost cause. Or to put it in market terms, the price of stocks goes up and down, fluctuating according to a plethora of factors. A big swing in the price of a stock is a comedy, a drama, a tragedy or a non-event, according to your involvement or perception of it.

Care About the Money

Many spiritual seekers may have felt that money is somehow not spiritual, or is less spiritual than other things. Therefore, they "don't care about money." When I hear that, I ask, "Does money care about you?"

Think about that statement for a minute. If something's not important to you, it's not important to you. If you don't care about money, it is probably not growing or circulating in your life. It's not a big part of your life because you don't care about it.

Would you say, "I don't care about food?" Or "I don't care about my body?" Or "I don't care about air?" Probably not! Money, food, bodies and oxygen are all just material things. But in an interconnected universe, material things symbolize spiritual realities. On this material plane, bodies, food, money and actions *are* important and worth caring about at their proper level.

Master teacher Byron Katie often challenges her students to dismantle their ego-identities with questions like, "Who would you be without your personal stories?" You'd think she wouldn't care about the physical world. But when she was asked, "What's the point, then? Why do you even brush your teeth?" She replied, "I brush my teeth because I like to chew." Do you like to thrive, serve, create and share your gifts? If so, in this dimension you need food, air and money!

I've never heard a person with real financial peace, freedom, and abundance who did not care about the money itself. When wealthy, healthy, prosperous people talk about money as a tool or a vehicle that supports exchange or creation, they speak with respect. They may say, "I don't worry about money," or "I'm not obsessed with money" or "It's not just about the money." There's a very different energy than, "I don't care about money."

What Game Are You Playing?

In the meaning you choose to create about money, you decide what the game is. What is winning? What is losing? Who sets the rules? Can they change? Who are the players? What's the point? What does it mean? This is where you create your answer to the question, "What's the money for?"

The meaning you choose about money touches the concepts of winning and losing, good and evil, and life and death. Money has a certain heroic, tragic and important energy that we as a culture have assigned to it. Beliefs about money are often complex and arise from a variety of influences.

On a personal level, the meaning you make about money has much to do with your inherent personal value. What you believe about money often is connected to what you value about yourself. "Am I enough?" "Am I lovable?" "Am I worthy?" "Am I whole?" "Do I have what it takes?" "Will I be supported?"

Conditioning

The sources of belief include some of the following:

- Current, conscious desires.
- The sum of our personal family and social conditioning.
- The current collective beliefs of the human race.
- The subconscious beliefs generated by our individual past experiences.

You have been influenced in your financial thinking by parents, siblings, caregivers, teachers, playmates and peers. This conditioning can affect you in ways you may or may not be aware of. Who hasn't suddenly realized that he or she is doing or saying something exactly like his or her parents?

- "My mother never knew anything about money, so as a woman, I certainly don't."
- "I've made numerous of mistakes in the stock market."
- "I never learned this."
- "I never had an opportunity."
- "People who are [fill in the blank] like I am can't get ahead."

In the practice of inquiry that I will introduce in this chapter, you will list and examine your parents' dominant beliefs about money, themselves and the world. It is important for you to be totally honest with yourself in this section. Only when we can honestly identify our beliefs can we change them!

Subconscious Beliefs

You see, sometimes someone *says* they want a certain kind of wealth experience, but don't manifest that experience because of hidden beliefs. Humans are deep, complex beings. In addition to our conscious beliefs, we have subconscious ideas, perceptions and thoughts about ourselves, money and our lives. These subconscious beliefs are a part of our souls, which we discover over a lifetime of spiritual practice and self-inquiry.

Collective Beliefs

We're also affected by collective beliefs held by groups at social, cultural, religious and ethnic levels. Think about all the images about money and value you've encountered on television, in music, in movies, in books, on the Internet and more. Those images and your reactions and involvement with them over your lifetime are part of the meaning you create about money today.

For example, a disempowering powerful energy around money shows up as unhealthy competition in our culture. This is the belief that winning means exploiting, dominating and killing your opponent so that there's a victor and a victim. Competition that is dominant or exploitative is a symbol of being out of our oneness, where we are all connected. When you truly understand that we are all in this money game together, you put together deals that maximize everyone's gifts, talents and offerings in which everyone makes a fantastic return.

Beliefs about Your Value

As human beings, we hold the meaning we make about ourselves through the human ego. The ego is our personality, history and identity, which keeps us separate from other people.

Identity related to our history and our future can be positive. Some of the stories we tell can be motivating and encouraging. For example, Wendy started a network marketing business. After six months, the revenue was not where she hoped. She told herself, "I've always been successful at things I've learned and done. I can be successful here." There is something about the integrity of having a sense of personality and creating self-esteem from the mental, emotional and physical level that is very gratifying.

The danger comes when you believe that *your* history and personality are the source of *your* supply, rather than the unlimited, eternal supply of *God*. You feel separate and scared without the larger, spiritual context, especially if your history is one of struggle, lack or failure.

In *Illusions*, author Richard Bach's main character counsels his young friend, "If you argue for your limitations, they're yours." Once you create stories about who you are, you get attached to those stories. It threatens the ego to ask, "Who would I be without this story?" When you have a spiritual context for your life, you have a foundation of who you are that allows you to break past the ideas of the ego.

A Counseling Perspective

Working with a coach, counselor or mastermind group can help you discover, transform and choose the money meaning that best serves you. Before looking at the practices of inquiry, healing and co-creation, here are specific examples of how beliefs around money can transform. Angela C. Montano is a brilliant and loving full-time spiritual counselor. She is dedicated to witnessing the wholeness, freedom and possibilities within her clients. She assists them in making meaning that celebrates who they truly are. She comments on the meaning people choose about money.

"I've certainly worked with people who have had all kinds of different challenges with money. There is a whole group of people who have a challenge around how to get money. Then there is that group of people who have the challenge of how to grow money. And there are people who have a great deal of money but feel undeserving of it for various reasons.

With getting money, the consciousness from a spiritual perspective has to be shifted. It's having a realization that money is not something that is outside of us. You can listen to that statement and hear the absurdity. Certainly I am here, and I am this person. I am in a body, and money is this medium of exchange. It is something that I need, and it is outside of me. To feel at one with money, there's an internal shift that has to happen.

I was one of these people. I tried to figure out how to get money. I put all this money that I had in my purse, car or home out on my desk. It was various denominations, 20's, 5's, and 10's. I might have had a 100 dollar bill. I stared at the money, and as I looked, I noticed how I felt and what thoughts I had. I was surprised to find that I was almost getting high. I saw that I thought if I had enough money, everything would be okay. If I have enough of this and get sick, it'll be okay because I'll have all the care I need to get well. Even if I get sick and I can't get well, at least I'll be able to die in some comfortable place with enough pain medication. I thought that if I have enough money and never find love in my life then it will be okay because at least I'll be able to wear nice clothes, live in a beautiful place, and travel as I choose.

The great shift was to "How do I trust God with everything the same way I was so easily trusting money with everything?" With God I have everything I need – that's what it was about. And that's a bit of a jump because money is visible, and my experience of God is an internal, invisible knowing.

Because I gave all the power I had given to money to God, I was then able to develop this sense that I have everything I need. If God needs to show up as money, then it will happen. If God needs to show up as a new friend, then that will happen. If God needs to show up as a great real estate deal, that will happen, too. I'm placing my faith in a higher power that I'm intrinsically one with. For me, money stopped being something I needed to get that was outside of me. The beliefs to empower us are things like, "Money is god in action," and "I am one with an abundant universe."

There are people who can just manifest money with a snap of their fingers. They can lose one job and have a better paying job before you know it. Money comes to them easily. But accumulating wealth and allowing that money to grow are problems.

Challenges with managing money are also very interesting. For those people, there is a compulsion or addiction to releasing money, letting it go, and it's a problem with not having it. This creates a feeling that it's not okay for them to have money. They're happy to work for money, and they're happy to get money. They're also happy to release money.

These people may receive a large sum of money and then spend thousands of dollars to send their whole family to Europe. They feel generous and wonderful, but when they get back, there's nothing. The quality in consciousness that has to be realized is one of deserving. "I deserve to enjoy my life." It's an awareness of what it means to be a container of good. It's working with the idea of letting their money work for them.

Allowing their money to work for them and to have the experience of having money is being able to contain energy. From there, you're giving from the overflow. It's having the capacity to hold. When we close off the exit ramps, we let that money flow. We let the energy flow, then something happens that's much greater than we could ever imagine.

It reminds me of the idea of compounding. If you save $100 per month at 10% interest from the time you are born, by the time you're 50 you will have $1,459,604. During those 50 years, you will have put in only $60,000, which is less than many people earn in a year. Yet that small sum will have earned $1,399,604 in interest without your lifting a finger. It's being comfortable with the expansion of good.

There's also an immaturity in spending whatever money you have, because you're not really valuing all that money can be. Financial maturity is a greater awareness of the value that money has to work for you, to accumulate, and to expand. For those clients, we ask, "Who do I need to be in order to step into that bigger space?"

Each person I've worked with has a unique story regarding money issues. Some people have stories about being responsible for their families. In their minds they never get a chance to accumulate wealth for themselves because they're paying their mother's rent or their sister's mortgage. They gain a great deal of value from being seen as the giver. But they don't hold any for themselves.

Others I've worked with believe that they don't have anything to show for all their work and the tremendous amount of money they've made because they're investing in their businesses. But they're not really investing in their businesses the way they think they are. They're giving their money away. They can't keep it. Containment is the problem that rises to the surface.

The third challenge is feeling guilty for having a large sum of money. Maybe these people do contain their money, and they may have great portfolios which are getting good returns. They own real estate that's going up in value. They have plenty, and perhaps they don't even have to work, but they are still not living a life of wealth because they don't feel they deserve it. I've seen this story many times with inherited wealth. "I didn't earn it so I don't deserve it. I feel bad about myself because I'm rich. But I'm really the poor rich child because I'm poor in the sense of really having ownership over money." I've also seen this with people who make big salaries and maybe don't even like the work they do. They make a great deal of money and feel like they don't deserve it because it's not their passion. They dismiss the expertise they have.

Or someone has a spouse who makes good salary and they don't. I've seen instances of wage-earning spouses who feel their spouses deserve money because they're partners, but the ones receiving it don't feel that they deserve it. That's an issue of, "What is my source?" "Is my source God, or is my source this money?" Somehow they know the money isn't their source, but they're treating it like it is. They don't know how to receive. What I work on with these clients is trust in God.

I also work with people relating to the idea of karma. Right now in your lifetime you've come into this money, and this is where you are now. How do you live fully in this space with this good fortune? What choices can you make that are the most dynamic, life enhancing and uniquely expressive choices? We must work through a person's reluctance to be creative.

What they are being given with their money is an opportunity to be creative, and instead, they're reluctant. There's fear of making a mistake, or they have a feeling of unworthiness. "I don't really deserve to be seen or heard, so I'm not going to use my money to express myself."

Another type of person is someone I call the "money monk." The money monk has guilt and negative feelings about having money. It's a belief that money is corrupt. It's bad to have money, to want money, and to value money. Money is somehow less spiritual than valuing a sunset, a flower or a beautiful blue sky. This individual needs to develop the idea that money can be as holy as any other thing we might think of as a creation. We certainly see money do great things on this planet – educating children, caring for the planet and building great cathedrals. The money monk must release his or her prejudice about money and be very watchful of that tendency to create a self-image that says, "I'm about these spiritual things, and I'm not about money."

I've also seen some really extraordinary things happen for people with money when they combine their sense that God is their source.

One woman came to me who was bouncing checks left and right. She was a single mother with four children. Everything had gotten out of *hand. She was spending above her means and incurring these rather large check charges. We ended up looking at the money she had, and figured out how much she actually had to spend on everything. I remember that we reduced her entertainment budget for one week with four children to $15. You can't even take four children to a movie for $15! But she decided to stick to it, and they ended up going to wonderful free summer concerts. They had more fun than ever. A relative ended up paying for a trip for them to take that was a gift. That had never occurred before.*

Within about four months, this woman got a new job making three times more money than she originally made. It was a combination of honoring the limit of what you have while knowing the limitlessness of God. When people can do those two things at the same time, great things can happen.

So we must always remember to both honor our personal limits and recognize God's infinite nature. If we just trust the limit, then we create a very small space. We don't live in any kind of possibility. We drone on with our little tiny bit. Or we go to the other extreme and we spend beyond our needs and don't respect money. This woman had never gone to free concerts in the city before. That was a miracle to her, to find all these great things that were always there for her to enjoy, not to mention a better job. When you can honor the limits of what you have while honoring the limitlessness of God, that is "the Midas touch." That's when miracles happen.

Practices and Processes

How can you create more empowered money and get in the game you want to play? Build on what's working, heal what's not, and commit to growing. Once you initiate even the smallest shift in direction, momentum builds and flows where you are headed.

You decide you want to author the stories of your life about money rather than unconsciously act out the scripts of social conditioning or collective beliefs.

The processes of inquiry, healing and co-creation include respect for your personality, your experiences of conditioning, the influence of collective beliefs, and the mysteries of your subconscious. All of the elements that make up who you are and, therefore, the meaning you make of your money financial life.

Inquiry, Healing, Co-Creation

The process of choosing new meaning includes inquiry, healing and co-creation. Although the process is described in sequence, it's a flow of energy - a cycle, like breathing.

In this process, you discover the thoughts, emotional reactions and perceptions that are with you. You neutralize or dissolve the beliefs that are not empowering to you. You empower the beliefs that link to your vision and energize the goals you want. You re-focus that energy on what you want to experience.

Inquiry

Inquiry is conscious conversation with yourself. Inquiry is a commitment to self-reflection for the purpose of discovering the thoughts, feelings and perceptions you have about the reality you serve, the games you play, and the goals you achieve. Assessing the content of your past consciousness and seeing what is still operating today is powerful.

There are many spiritual psychological and personal growth systems that involve the practice of honest self-inquiry. The twelve-step programs like Alcoholics Anonymous include steps four through nine, which are for cleaning your inner house. Confession of sins is a practice in many religions. Coming to terms with what's happening is a major element of good psychotherapy. Inquiry is about fearlessly facing your true self.

In some ways, our Western culture is more comfortable with intimate details of weight, illness, sex life or addictions than with financial choices, behaviors and dollar amounts. People can be eccentric and secretive about money. Sometimes, behaviors we don't understand or feel we can't change become secrets. And secrets can be shameful. Inquiry is a safe way to uncover what's there.

Hillary's Inquiry

Hillary is a bright, creative woman with a talent for designing greeting cards for animal lovers. But she hasn't always known how to harness this talent to succeed. After struggling with business and accounting classes, she dropped out of college. Over the next few years, she amassed numerous loans as she tried to get started in the design business. During this time, she also experienced a bad relationship that was chaotic and volatile. She found herself alone with $36,000 in credit card debt, frustrated by her circumstances. The meaning she made for her life was the feeling of, "I am unworthy. I am incompetent. It's not fair. Things don't work out for me, and what I'm doing isn't important."

In inquiry, Hillary worked with a counselor, on her own, and with a support group to delve deeper into her feelings to see her primary belief of, "I'm not valuable." She realized how certain behaviors, attitudes and choices affirmed that basic belief in her life.

She committed to forgive herself and started to create beliefs and habits that reflected her self-value. She asked friends to stop her if she made self-deprecating comments. She no longer gave her work away for free. She no longer lent money to a boyfriend who wasn't working. Understanding how the belief that she was not valuable was manifesting itself in her life empowered her to choose new meaning.

It is not hard to find out what you believe about money and what meaning you have made about yourself. The simple beliefs inventory on the next page is a way to discover your past and present beliefs and to move into the process of living from the wholeness and freedom that is who you really are.

The Money Keys Practice: Money Beliefs Inventory

Prepare:
- Set aside thirty to sixty minutes.
- Create an inspiring, undistracted environment.

Center:
- Take three deep breaths, in through the nose and out through the nose and mouth.
- Consciously open to your connection with the divine.
- You can say "I surrender" out loud.

Write:

- Allow yourself to write without correction or evaluation about the following topics:

- My family conditioning:

- What did my parents and caregivers say, do and believe about money, work, worth, wealth, rich, poor, taxes, fairness, savings, etc.?

- What were the most painful or memorable moments, sayings or events from my childhood about money?

- Social conditioning:

- What did my religion, neighborhood, ethnic group, friends and schoolmates say, do, believe, feel or choose around money, work, worth, rich, and poor?

- Collective beliefs:

- What characters in the media or entertainment or teachers do I most emulate in their beliefs about money?

- Who are my heroes or villains and why?

- Right now, when it comes to money, I feel:
  _____ (happy, sad, angry, jealous, worried, hopeful, tired, resentful, ashamed, joyous, etc.)

- Right now, when it comes to money, I am:
  _____ (competent, learning, a fool, a victim, a leader, skilled, smart, stupid, and so forth.)

- Money is _____ (easy, hard, tough, flowing, not there, mysterious, etc.)

- When it comes to money, people are _____ (fair, jealous, crazy, honest, cheaters, nutty, etc.)

- If you just looked at my financial life without any inside knowledge, you'd probably think _____.
- Anything else? Take a deep breath and see what else is going on in your thoughts and feelings about money.

Blessing:

- Congratulations. You did it! In the healing process, you'll have the option of sharing your inventory with another person. For now, let yourself feel and release any emotions that are present. Say something like, "I'm grateful to be aware. I trust myself. I am one with wholeness. Thank you, life. All is well."

Reward yourself:

- Do something wonderful and positive for yourself.

Healing

Healing is releasing the "hold" of false ideas of limitation and separation. It's not fixing brokenness or making goodness out of bad. Healing is letting go. Appreciate yourself for your honesty and accuracy in doing your inventory. You can see how the past has served you, and you must be willing to surrender that which no longer serves you before you can embrace something that does.

You can consciously find an outlet for healthy expression of the emotional energy tied up with your beliefs. For some, it is journaling; others are supported by working with a compassionate counselor or friend.

What feelings have you attached to money? Is there anger, sadness, grief, guilt, shame, fear or anxiety? Is there joy, happiness, possibility, bliss, excitement, empowerment and delight?

Experiencing the emotion in a non-judgmental and conscious way allows you to let go. It doesn't have to take a long time or even be understood completely by the intellect. Sometimes, having a good cry or burning the angry letter to a deceased parent or an old boss is all it takes. The help of a good counselor, a coach or a spiritual companion can be useful. That individual can create a safe place to hear and witness the healing.

To your subconscious self, letting go of an old belief about money can feel like a death. And it is. An old idea is dying. If you mix up the idea with your identity, it can be terrifying to let go. That's why you may sometimes sabotage yourself or go back to old ways of being, even when you say you want to move on. It's not that you don't know better; some shadowy, hidden part of you is fighting for its life. Just realizing this can free you from the guilt of struggling with old identities. Old beliefs can feel like who you are even if they're not true. Having compassion for yourself is essential to the grieving process.

Speaker and author Debbie Ford is a master at teaching the value of looking for the gifts in the shadow. The shadow may hide the parts of you that you'd call ugly, but always behind the ugly is the beautiful, powerful you. The truth does set you free. The gift that is brought forward by identifying a belief like, "I'm not worthy," can be an awesome release of power and energy. Who would you be without this belief? Yes, a part of you dies, but something is born. Possibility in you wakes up! You develop skills and capacities that serve you. The more you know of yourself, the more capacity for expressing the creative source you can access.

Forgiveness

You use the inquiry process to get accurate about the facts. Then you express and release those emotions. Healing continues into forgiveness.

Healing negative or limiting beliefs about money requires that you release judgment about your money circumstances and the money circumstances of others. If you have debts or bankruptcy or struggles from divorce, consumer spending, business ventures, job loss, loans, illness or investments, it can be tempting to look for what went wrong, who's to blame and what to do about it. But there's no peace, power or possibility in resentment, blame or rage, all of which keep you locked in the past.

Forgiveness is choosing to release attachment, energy and connection to the past and to be empowered, free and giving in the present. Forgiveness is the release of judgment about yourself and others. Sometimes there's resistance to forgiving.

Here is a quick list of what forgiveness is not:

1) Forgiveness is not condoning what happened or making excuses.
2) Forgiveness is not reconciliation with the person or institution.
3) Forgiveness is not giving up boundaries or failing to take self-protective actions.
4) Forgiveness is not weakness.

Forgiveness happens in the present moment. You activate your own freedom to perceive yourself and your life from a loving, compassionate and empowered point of view. You take responsibility for and choose the meaning you make now.

Forgiveness is not God's responsibility. God, the infinite presence of all love, power, supply and truth, doesn't condemn or judge. Therefore, God doesn't forgive. Forgiveness is the human process of aligning yourself with what is true and compassionately releasing what is not.

Your hurt surrounding money is often connected to traps of scarcity and superstition. You may worry that there's not enough to go around or that the limited supply can't be replaced. You might resent governments, bosses, IRS, the economy, corporations, banks, lovers or family that you feel control your money life. When you simply don't believe you're capable and empowered to change things, you can become angry and feel like a victim with your money.

Forgiving others means you let go of the agreement that they or their actions have power over you. Look at the money deeds of others. They don't always think, feel or act in a way you think is right. What do you need to release and forgive? Who has hold over you? Many of the popular twelve-step programs say that holding resentment is like drinking poison and hoping the other person will die. Forgiving others frees you from the mistaken idea that others have control over your well-being.

A Metaphysical Perspective on Forgiveness

Many people operate under the spiritual misperception that when we forgive another, we are doing something for them. In reality, all forgiveness is a gift we give to ourselves.

Rev. Jennifer Hadley is a passionate student and teacher of the metaphysical lessons of *A Course in Miracles*. She shares an important perspective on the practice of forgiveness.

"A Course in Miracles teaches us that we cannot have what we aren't willing to give. Because all minds are joined, everyone can "hear" everything I'm thinking on a spiritual level. There's no place to hide.

When I withhold forgiveness, I am saying that I believe others are unworthy of compassion. If I judge one person unworthy of my compassion, then I must absolutely be unworthy as well. What is true for one is true for all. Within moments of a judgment, I will, I must, experience a sense of unworthiness in one way or another, whether I'm aware of it or not.

There is that within me that knows that all is one. So, when I cannot forgive, when I judge or take offense, I am insisting on living from a belief that the divine is not in everything, but only in some things. Since my spirit knows this is not true, unforgiveness immediately causes a rift in my being. I am then choosing the judgment over forgiveness, fear over love and insanity over God.

Judgment is the refusal to forgive. This is the hidden cause of the vast majority of pain and suffering. The antidote is always available. Forgive and be free. You can start right now by forgiving yourself for having chosen judgment a moment ago and choosing compassion for yourself right now. Now you are free. The world appears more loving, safe and supportive to you because you have changed your perception of it. For the feeling of love, prosperity and freedom to prevail, these qualities must prevail in your mind.

Through a deep practice of forgiveness, you are profoundly supported by the invisible and therefore you have much to give. You make the world a more loving, safe and supportive place for all."

Here is the next practice, an opportunity for healing and forgiveness.

The Money Keys Practice: Healing and Forgiveness

Invite support:

- Choose a loving, confidential, trustworthy prosperity partner, coach, counselor or friend to sit with you in the *healing* process.

Prepare:

- Set aside an hour or two together.
- Create or visit an inspiring, undistracted environment.

Center:

- Take three deep breaths, in through the nose and out through the nose and mouth.
- Consciously open to your connection with the divine.
- You can say "I surrender" out loud.

Share your inventory:

- Read or talk through all the stories, the secrets and the beliefs from your money beliefs inventory.
- Have your partner listen with love and compassion, with no need to fix or give advice.

What are the themes?

- On a separate piece of paper, capture the major themes or beliefs that are still with you today about money, you and the world.

Release the emotion and the past:

- Cry, laugh, yell, etc.
- Let the hurt child within you have his/her say as needed.

Let it go:

- Physically let go.
- Burn the papers of the inventory.
- Bury the inventory in the ground, toss the energy into the ocean, shred the old pictures, give away the mementos, etc.

Choose to forgive:

- Consciously release the judgments about you and all those involved.
- For each self-judgment, write,"I forgive myself for judging myself as _____. "
- Read it out loud with your partner.
- Have your partner respond by saying: "You are forgiven."

See wholeness:

- Choose to see yourself and everyone as spiritually whole and one with the higher power.
- Say a prayer such as:

  Holy Spirit, I offer up every fact, every person, every thought, every emotion, every choice, everything about my self, my money and my life to you. With your loving, gracious, giving truth, I surrender into thinking, seeing, feeling and acting from my wholeness. Help me to know my truth and to serve it in everyone. I give thanks for every insight and gift. Thank you.

Get the lesson:

- Write down what you learned, discovered, revealed or gained from this experience.

- Write down what you truly want to think, feel and believe.

Blessing:

- You did it!

- Say, "Thank you life,"

- Bless and thank your partner.

Celebrate:

- Reward yourself in a loving and encouraging way.

Co-Creation

We are creative by nature, and, because we are one with the divine, we create out of its image and likeness, which is endless in expression. We co-create our lives with the divine by our thoughts, language, emotion and perception.

Thought generates emotional reaction, which, upon repetition and focus, becomes belief. Language articulates belief. Attention, intensity and the selective perception of evidence reinforce our perceptions and become our reality. You can deliberately and consciously choose the direction, content and energy of the beliefs you wish to empower.

Spiritual teacher Bob Proctor talks about the conscious mind as a guardian. Nothing will come into your awareness unless it is either consciously selected by you or unconsciously allowed to come in. Taking in ideas and the repetition of them, particularly if they are linked up with an emotional reaction and a certain level of physical response or intensity, become stories. If repeated, these stories become "real."

How do you choose new beliefs about your money life that mentally empower and emotionally involve you? You focus energy onto specific truths you want to empower.

For every spiritual quality, there's a continuum of expression. If you have been ignorant, that is just the limited experience of wisdom. If you have been hoarding, you're not fully expressing affluence and circulation. Lack of time is a call for right action. Anxiety calls for peace. Fear is an invitation for freedom and faith.

Strengthening thoughts and beliefs about money with techniques like affirmation and prayer is powerful. Affirmations are present tense positive statements you can genuinely believe are so. These statements capture the essence of the game you are playing, the roles you are taking, the wins you want, and the outcomes you are sharing.

Create affirmative statements that neutralize negative beliefs. If you have unconsciously believed that people from your ethnic class can't really move past their place in life, you could neutralize that belief with an affirmation, "People just like me can make money and make a difference."

Affirmations can also be specific to the new beliefs to which you're committed. For example: "I will be grateful every morning." "I will take action to increase my income." "I am able to have a positive emotional relationship with my spouse." "I am a powerful contributor to the consciousness of wealth on this planet." "I create opportunity and possibility through my work and my investments." Involve mental, emotional, soulful and energetic aspects of who you are in the money game you play.

Prayer is a powerful practice for aligning your thinking, emotions, perceptions and habits with serving a spiritual reality of wholeness. Affirmative prayer is a prayer of faith. We speak not so much to God asking for things as from our awareness that God is our source. It's also vital to use imagery, music, art or nature in our *co-creation* to get emotionally involved with the objects, goals and visions we desire.

The Money Keys Practice: Co-Creation

Prepare:

- Set aside thirty to sixty minutes for the first *co-creation* session and then ten to fifteen minutes daily for anchoring it into your beliefs.

- Create an inspiring, undistracted environment.

Center:

- Take three deep breaths, in through the nose and out through the nose and mouth.

- Consciously open to your connection with the divine.

- You can say "I surrender" out loud.

Expand your vision of what's possible:

- Revisit your wealth vision.

- Write, draw or visualize the essence and ideas of what you desire in money and its meaning in your life.

Know what beliefs you are choosing:

- Remember the question, "What must I be in consciousness to serve the vision?"

- Now that you have released the emotional energy and judgments from past beliefs, what beliefs about yourself, your money and the world do you choose?

- Write out each of the following and fill in the blanks:

- In my money life, I am _____(free, generous, powerful, creative, excited, prosperous, gracious, talented, etc.).

- Money is _____ (flowing easily to me, naturally available, plentiful and powerful, a resource for all, etc.).

- My work/business/projects is/are _____ (contributing to the world, etc.).

- The world/the universe/God supports and celebrates me by _____ (providing   for my needs, reflecting my wholeness, etc.).

- My money game is _____(describe the game, the players, the roles, the results, the fun of your game).

Empower your vision:

- Using art, images, symbols, etc. create a visual reminder of your vision and the beliefs it reflects.

Create a daily practice:

- Make a recording of chants, songs or instrumental music of five to fifteen minutes that helps you feel emotionally involved with your vision.

- Set aside ten to fifteen minutes each day and do a ritualized practice:

- Listen to the music while picturing you in the vision.

- Repeat the affirmations while looking at the pictures.

- Take a walk and connect with the symbols of your vision.

Pray:

- Your vision is a co-creation with you and the infinite presence of wholeness.

- Say a prayer to bless your vision:

"How grateful I am for wholeness. I give thanks for living in a unified reality that is all peace, all supply, all information, all resource and all energy. I remember myself. I _____, am at one with this generous, friendly, powerful universe. The Laws of Unity, Cause and Effect, and Circulation are operating for my good and the good of all. I live in the beliefs that life is for me and that I am a powerful giver and receiver. I circulate good in everything I am and everything I do. My businesses, projects, investments and actions reflect the freedom, love and truth of life. I am grateful for the beliefs that I am building. Thank you, life; I surrender to you. It is good. All is well".

Celebrate:

- Reward yourself for being in positive co-creation with life!

Creating new meaning that is mentally empowering and emotionally involving means staying awake. Don't fall asleep. Don't allow the seduction or hypnosis of social conditioning, past experiences or collective consensus to pull you back! Authoring a new story and new meaning about money requires desire and discipline. It's worth it for you to live a life of wholeness, freedom and growth. You deserve it!

Your desire to experience real financial power that is spiritually uplifting, mentally empowering and emotionally involving doesn't only create good for you; it serves everybody. When you have a sense of separation, it doesn't just affect the ones who seem to be the victims. If you cheat, you are cheated. If you manipulate, you are manipulated. You get out what you put in. There is no good that is good for some people that cannot at some level be good for all. Conversely, when you create from prosperity, flow and generosity, you contribute to everyone.

Chapter Five Review

Questions for Reflection

1) What are my beliefs about how the universe operates and the *Law of Cause and Effect*?

2) What has happened to me in the past that I can now see that I attracted or created through my beliefs?

3) What is my value? What do I believe to be true about my worth and worthiness?

Ideas for Action

1) Co-creation party. Come as you'll be!

- Host a party where you and your guests come as yourselves, in the wealthy, generous, prosperous roles, goals and beliefs you are co-creating.

- Dress, act, eat, decorate, share, bring, speak, dance and mingle as "owner of a high end doggie daycare" or "giver of $200,000 in youth scholarships" or "creator of a new line of environmentally friendly cleaning products" or whatever your dream may be.

- Have everyone introduce themselves, share their dreams in present tense, and present any gifts or offers they want to circulate.

Tools

Visit **www.themoneykeys.com/tools** to listen to *A Money Game Worth Playing*. This recorded conversation among a Prosperity MasterMind group is all about creating wins in the money game.

Review *The Money Keys Recommended Resources* to contact a spiritual coach like Angela C. Montano who can work with you to transform your beliefs.

Chapter Six

Habits: Get Into the Flow of Giving and Receiving

"The most powerful force in the

universe is compound interest."

– Albert Einstein

Chapter Six

Your money map includes actions, habits, decisions and choices around the way you earn, give, share, save and invest money. Every action you take with money makes a difference. Every bill you pay, purchase you make, debt you incur, gift you give, investment you choose, business you run, and dollar you save can become a conscious habit that positively contributes to the way you experience money, as well as the results you get.

If you've developed a regular spiritual practice and prosperous vision, you're feeling connected to wholeness. If you've consciously chosen to build a belief system that acknowledges your financial freedom, you're feeling more empowered around money and the meaning it has in your life.

Integrating a reality worth serving and a game worth playing into the daily habits in your money life can be really fun! For some, it means the drudgery of bill-paying becoming a practice of sacred blessing. For others, it means making automatic deposits into a play money account each month. Others take a class on stock trading, learn a software program for leveraging the equity in their home, or get a real estate license. What habits will help you achieve your goals?

Struggling Is Not Necessary

Victoria Castle, author of *The Trance of Scarcity*, states that, "If struggling were the way to get there, we'd all be there by now." The money trap of survival mode makes us busy, frantic and moving, but not usually in the flow of the natural, balanced and graceful lives many people want. Although busy-ness is common in our culture, it's not always productive. Most people who want to be rich really want to be able to breathe, relax and live freely. Struggling in the quicksand of busy, distracted, fast-paced living can spill over into your financial actions and behaviors.

Getting Into the Flow

The nature of life is flow and circulation. Energy, which is the fundamental component of all creation, flows. Energy is always available and always creating. The origin of the word affluence is the Latin word *affluere*, which means "to flow toward." The spiritual principle that teaches us the power of the flow is the *Law of Circulation*.

The Law of Circulation

The *Law of Circulation* is based on the spiritual idea that we live in an abundant, creative universe of infinite energy that is always flowing. The nature of life is giving and receiving. All of life is circulation. What we give, we are. What we give, we experience. What we give, we receive. There is always more of that which is infinite to give and receive.

Many wonderful images symbolize the *Law of Circulation*. Breathing is a beautiful example of effortless and natural circulation. We inhale to take in oxygen. Magnificent things happen with the oxygen in our bodies to keep us vital and thriving. We exhale, releasing the carbon dioxide that is no longer needed. The flow requires that we take in and give out. If we stop breathing, we die. If we hoard all our inhalations without exhaling, we can't go on.

What we do not need, the carbon dioxide is essential to plants. There's a natural, intelligent flow at work in our bodies and on our planet that represents the intelligence of the divine.

When we circulate money, we give out symbols of supply. We share energy. That energy supports the people and things with whom we've shared. In turn, the energy is converted into goods, services, ideas and offerings that circulate to others. When we're in the flow with the circulation of money, we align ourselves with the natural affluence of life.

Giving and Receiving

The movement of money is a symbol of giving and receiving, and facilitates the circulation of supply. In an infinite universe, there is no need to hoard or withhold. There is no need to be cautious in giving or receiving. It is a spiritual axiom that if you want to have something, you need to give it. If you want to receive more love, you need to give more love. If you want more spiritual connection, you need to give more energy and attention to spiritual connection. If you want more time for yourself, you need to put more time into your schedule.

Do you want to immediately get into the flow of circulation? Start giving. You'll see that the practices presented in this chapter are all based on proactively stepping into the flow by giving something of yourself. When you give, you receive, and you participate in the possibilities of expansion.

Since all is one, you are giving from the oneness. You are receiving from the oneness. You give to yourself when you give, and you receive from yourself when you receive.

Inspired Action

Where do you start? Do you start by changing your thoughts or changing your actions? You can do either or both. In the Science of Mind teaching, it's said, "Change your thinking, change your life." It's also true that if you change your life, your thoughts will catch up.

Cultivate spiritual awareness, select beliefs that empower you, and take action in the direction of your beliefs. The twelve-step programs are a great example of the idea to "change your actions and your thinking will change." Put down the drink, drugs or destructive behavior. Become abstinent. Then work on spiritual realizations and cleaning up your thinking. Changing the behavior builds the willingness and commitment for long-term growth.

In building a wealth consciousness and reality around qualities like wholeness, freedom and creativity, both approaches work. Acting generously by giving time and money contributes to generous thoughts and feelings. Feeling grateful for what you have and allowing generosity to flourish can lead you to give time and money. Another way to view this is change from the inside out (first thoughts and then behavior) and from the outside in (first behavior and then thoughts). In the late 1800's the psychologist William James described the outside-in process as "acting as if." That is, acting as if one already has those habits and those habits will develop.

The practices in this chapter build habits that contribute to serving a reality of wholeness and playing a money game of co-creation. The practices are blessing, serving, spiritual giving, managing the money flow and having a wealth expansion plan.

Blessing

"When you focus on being a blessing, God makes sure that you are always blessed in abundance."
– Joel Osteen

Giving your blessing is consciously directing thanks, well-being and attention onto the person, action or thing you bless. The concept of blessing is found in many traditions. The Hebrew Scriptures include the idea that blessing is the inheritance of divine grace, passed down to humanity. The Greek origin of blessing can be found in the verb *eulogew*, which means "to praise, to call down God's gracious power." Earth-based sacred practices include many rituals of giving thanks for the bounties and cycles of nature, which is a form of blessing.

Receiving well is graciously and consciously acknowledging all of the supply that currently flows to you. Acknowledging all the channels through which the infinite source flows to you is a form of giving a blessing. Salaries, interest, investments, gifts, retirement accounts, real estate, businesses, spouses, families and governments are all channels through which each of us is blessed. Whether you're buying or selling a latte or land, there's an exchange of value in every transaction. Blessing the transactions consciously is a way of circulating sacred energy.

Deliberately bless everyone and everything that comes into and out of your money life, regardless of your opinion about the person or the thing. Bless what you receive by saying "thank you" and "I bless you." Bless the checks you write, the bills you pay. Bless your vendors and customers. When you purchase something, bless the flow of all the goods, ideas and services with which you're in circulation. Bless the government. Some would say the government could really use your conscious blessing! Bless your ex. Bless your children. Bless the college, the loans and your creditors.

When you consciously participate in the flow, you start to feel like there's more to give and receive.

The Money Keys Practice: Blessing

Prepare:
- Turn away from external distractions.
- Find a comfortable, quiet place to sit and reflect.

Choose:
- What inflows and outflows, what channels in your financial life are the most important to bless?
- Where are you on auto-pilot?
- Whom, if anyone, do you resent or minimize?
- Choose where you bestow blessings.

> ## Bless:
> - Find a simple, repeatable way to bless the flows.
> - Say out loud or to yourself, "Thank you. I bless you. We are whole, and we are in the flow."

Serving

My happiest Christmas ever was in 1996. I was living in Los Angeles. I'd been single for several lifetimes, or so it felt, and I was lonely. Even though I had many friends, activities, and spiritual support groups, I didn't have a boyfriend, and I felt that lack.

On Christmas Day I wanted to get out of my own self-pity and see if I could be helpful to someone else. I went to Venice Beach, where I'd heard there was a spiritual group that was providing services at the Venice pier.

I found the check-in for volunteers. I chose to be of service in the clothing giveaway. Huge pallets of clothes that had been donated were being unpacked and spread out on enormous makeshift tables. Hundreds of people lined up and were told to walk past the tables and take just a few items at a time. Everyone had plastic grocery bags they filled to the brim. There was a great deal of excitement.

I found tremendous joy in helping the individuals who received donated clothes. I particularly loved helping the ladies. I waded through huge piles of clothes and found something that would be a really complementary color or style, or children's clothing that would really make the child smile. I completely threw myself into being the most creative, supportive, genuine and helpful personal shopper I could be.

At the end of the day, I was exhausted but excited to get out of my self-pity and into service. I felt a part of the experience and very grateful for everything I had. It was fun. I felt the heart-opening power of giving and receiving. What we give is what we get. That day, I wanted connection, and I found it by giving it away.

If you're lonely, get involved. If you want the world to be a healthier, greener or a safer place, get involved in the solutions and make a difference. Contribute your time and energy to projects, businesses and pursuits that inspire you.

Service is choosing to share your time, energy and talents with people and places where you experience qualities like wholeness, freedom and growth. Dr. Martin Luther King, Jr. once said, "Everybody can be great...because anybody can serve. You don't have to have a college degree to serve. You don't have to make your subject and verb agree to serve. You only need a heart full of grace. A soul generated by love."

The Money Keys Practice: Serving the Spirit

Prepare:
- Turn away from external distractions.
- Find a comfortable, quiet place to sit and reflect.

Choose:
- Where are you called to serve and in what way?
- What people, projects or institutions represent wholeness, circulation and inspiration to you?

- What skills, talents, resources or ideas do you feel called to share?
- Do any research you need to do.
- Select where you'll serve.

Serve:
- When you give your time, talents and energy, do it consciously.
- See those to whom you give and from whom you receive as part of the circulation of infinite wholeness.

Share:
- Let your prosperity partner, intimates or friends know what you learned, received and shared in service.

Spiritual Giving

If you want more money flowing into your life, you can activate a greater flow by giving of what you want. Tithing is giving ten percent of your income to the people, places and institutions that spiritually inspire you.

Reverend Diane Harmony, author of *5 GIFTS for an Abundant Life*, is one of the strongest teachers on tithing I know. She defines tithing as giving thanks for the 100 percent that comes in by leaving ten percent with our spiritual source.

In fact, the word tithe literally means "one tenth." The practice of giving one tenth can be traced back to ancient cultures that replanted ten percent of the crops in thanks for the gifts of heaven and earth. "Bringing the tithes into the storehouse" is an instruction from the Hebrew Scriptures. In the Christian New Testament, the teachings emphasize that tithing is not just a technical practice, but a way to circulate justice, love and faith in God. As a contemporary spiritual practice, spiritual giving is less about appeasing God and more about celebrating the generous flow of supply in which we participate.

How much should you give? Start where you are by giving some percentage or some portion of your inflow from a place of generosity and gratitude. This builds consciousness. You can grow from there up to ten percent, or more!

To whom do you give? Give to people or institutions that uplift you spiritually, that help you feel more connected to your source. I've tithed to spiritual communities, inspiring teachers, prayer partners, musicians and groups that provide spiritual services, like magazines or prayer lines.

How often do you give? Consistency builds discipline and faith. Some tithe every time there's inflow; others incorporate it into weekly or monthly money management.

What are the benefits of spiritual giving? When you consistently give a portion of your income from your gratitude for spiritual nourishment, you are fed. You activate your sense of generosity and prosperity.

Spiritual giving is different from charitable giving. In some traditional charitable giving, there are expectations about what the organization does with your money. When you tithe, you give freely, *without expectation*. Charitable giving can sometimes be done from a sympathetic motivation, a sense that your money will fix problems and help those who are in need. Spiritual giving is done from a sense of wholeness. You see yourself and all others as one with the flow, and your motivation for giving is gratitude and celebration. Charitable giving is wonderful! Many people incorporate both spiritual giving and charitable giving into their circulation. Both are powerful expressions of your abundance.

"How can I give ten percent when I don't have enough?" Sometimes people resist spiritual giving because of the money traps of scarcity and the superstitious belief that giving will diminish them. Start where you are. Give what you can *from* the idea that you and everyone are whole. You can't diminish yourself when you give from the infinite supply that flows through you and all of life.

When you participate in the joy of circulation, you magnify the joy. What is the benefit to you in spiritual giving? You'll receive what you expect, and I encourage you to expect a great deal! Spiritual giving allows you to be generous and grateful, which is a gift in itself. Spiritual giving builds faith in the wholeness of the source. You start giving and find there's more to give.

Tithing can be fun. I moved into tithing by first giving regularly, and I tracked what I was giving. At first I gave five percent, then seven percent, then tithed the full ten percent. After five years of tithing, I got a chance to stretch even more. I sold a condo and had a big gain, which meant I had a large amount of money to tithe.

But I started to feel nervous. Did I not want to tithe? Was I feeling over-responsible? After some meditation and prayer, I was reminded that God is my source and always will be. There's nothing I can do to personally block the infinite abundance. Tithing got me here; I'm grateful for this flow, so let me start writing the checks!

One of the tithe checks I wrote was to an individual who had been a spiritual inspiration to me for years. It was the largest tithe check I had ever written. I blessed it and dropped it in the mail. Several days later I got a fabulous phone call from my spiritual friend, gasping for air, absolutely delighted and saying through the tears, "Thank you! Thank you so much for honoring me and honoring yourself with this tithe." Then we laughed out loud because God is good!

The next day I went to see one of my spiritual counseling clients. I walked in and sat down. I noticed there was an envelope on the little table between us. At the end of our session, my client looked deeply into my eyes, gave me a big smile, handed me the envelope and said, "This is for you." I said thank you and put the envelope in my purse.

Driving away, I wondered about that envelope. I opened it up. Holy mackerel! It was the largest single tithe I had ever received! I gasped, my eyes filled with tears, and I started to laugh. God is really good! I felt so grateful to receive this tithe. I was completely comfortable receiving it. I was also happy for my client. We are all whole. Everyone prospered.

The Money Keys Practice: Spiritual Giving

Prepare:
- Turn away from external distractions.
- Find a comfortable, quiet place to sit and reflect.

Choose:

- What inflows are you ready to spiritually honor by leaving a portion with your source? Select the inflows and a method for tracking.

- What percentage will you give? A tenth as a tithe? More? Less?

- How frequently will you give?

- Where are you spiritually nourished? What people, institutions or programs help you feel a greater communion with your source?

Give:

- Send or give your gift with love, gratitude and submission.

Receive:

- Look for all the ways your spiritual giving makes you feel more prosperous, generous and free.

Managing the Money Flow

How you spend, track and organize your money reflects the reality you're serving, the game you're playing and the growth and goals you desire. It's important to understand how you manage your money, even if you have a spouse, partner, family member, accountant or someone else who does the mechanics.

People who have respect for and interest in the food, water and nutrients they put into their bodies probably know the source and content of what they ingest. Do you have the same level of information and confidence about what is happening with your money?
The discussion that follows will help you consciously manage your money flow.

Your Financial Foundation

Financial foundation is an orderly structure and process for the tactical, physical and practical circulation of money. Here are some practical elements of a strong foundation.

Begin with the personal or business assets you own or co-own. Know what they are and how they're valued, where the statements or titles of ownership are, when they were bought and for how much.

Go through the same process for liabilities, loans, credit cards or obligations for which you are individually or jointly responsible. What amounts do you owe, on what terms and interest rates, and to whom do you owe them?

What you own and what you owe are the components of a balance sheet. A balance sheet is a snapshot of your assets and liabilities at any given point in time. Assets represent the financial value of what you own; liabilities are the financial value of what you owe. The difference between what you own and what you owe is your net worth.

Net worth is not a static measure, and having a bigger number may not necessarily be your goal. In addition to the absolute number of your net worth, you will want to consider whether your assets are earning you money or costing you money. Assets can generate income or cash, like businesses or real estate, promissory notes, bonds that pay interest or stocks that pay dividends. Things you own such as cars, homes, clothes, electronics, art and hobby items can also cost money, time, energy and attention to maintain.

Your income (cash flow) statement shows the money that comes in and goes out and the channels through which it flows. Use your check stubs, annual W2s, checking and credit card accounts, accounting programs and income tax statements as ways to capture all the inflows and outflows.

If a balance sheet is a snapshot of your assets and liabilities at one point in time, an income statement is more like a movie about the circulation and money flow in the revenue. It shows how the movement of cash and energy flows through you, your businesses and your other legal business entities.

A strong financial foundation requires that you know where your income tax returns are for the past five to seven years. You need to understand what insurance you have or don't have, including auto, home, disability and life insurance. If you don't have a will or trust for the disbursement of your assets and liabilities when you die, you need to take action now as part of your foundation. You'll also want to assess the filing, information and tracking systems you have now and select the ones that work best for you.

Money is a form of energy. It can't flow where there is no space for it to flow. A stuffed closet won't fit more clothes. If there's no room in your garage, you can't park another car inside. If you're out every night dating three people, none of whom are "the one," where is your beloved going to fit in? If there's chaos and confusion in your financial accounts and affairs, more dollars won't fix it. With a financial foundation built on order, it is easy to add more to it.

Once you have a foundation of order and clarity, see how you handle the flow of money in and out. When money comes in, the first thing to do is bless it. After that, create your own money management system. Typical systems include setting aside specific percentages for spiritual giving, saving, financial investing, tax obligations, a contingency fund, long-term savings, daily spending and money for fun. There are many great teachers and references for money management systems, including the resources at **www.themoneykeys.com/tools.**

The Money Keys Practice: Managing the Money Flow

Prepare:
- Turn away from external distractions.
- Find a comfortable, quite place to sit and reflect.

Assess:
- Understand what your current money flow system and choices are.

Choose:
Where do you want to begin with categories and percentages in your money flow?

Categories:
Spiritual giving
Saving
Financial investing

Tax obligations
Contingencies
Debt reduction
Long term savings
Daily spending
Children
Legacy
Fun money

Percentages. (For the categories that are important to you, find a percentage and method for allocating money in each category that works for you).

Manage:

- On a regular basis, move or monitor the flow of money.
- Stay current and conscious.

Celebrate!

- As you experience more balance, possibility and power in the flow, celebrate in a way that feels great for you.

Growth and Expansion

Every successful entrepreneur, network marketer and investor I know has a passion for and commitment to expanding his or her own knowledge and capacity. Expanding yourself to a life of real financial power requires more than just accumulating information. Successful wealth education includes learning about the content of investments, business and finances, as well as developing skills and confidence to apply the information.

Learning happens in many ways: auditory, analytical, kinesthetic, emotional, practical and more. How do you learn best?

Practical learners like to experience things to understand them. Acquiring that first rental property teaches you things that you just can't learn in a seminar room.

Analytic learners want to read and absorb information completely before being thrown into action. Understanding the mortgage programs for that rental property thoroughly and running a contingency scenario on a spreadsheet helps an analytical learner.

Emotional learners want to hear real life stories in order to get inspired to make changes. Joining a real estate investment group and finding a mentor to learn from is powerful.

Auditory learners love to hear the words and ideas in order to really adopt them. Listening to CD set from a real estate guru helps an auditory learner incorporate ideas into their investment plans.

Think about the things you know about and do which make you feel confident. How have you developed mastery in those areas?

The following practice will help you be consistent and intentional as you continue to grow yourself while your grow your wealth.

The Money Keys Practice: Your Wealth Expansion Plan

Prepare:

- Turn away from external distractions.
- Find a comfortable, quiet place to sit and reflect.

Assess your growth needs:

- What methods and types of learning experiences are best for you?

  > Seminars
  > Books
  > Audio
  > Video
  > Digital courses
  > Group learning
  > Projects
  > Mentors
  > Reflection

- What content topics are most important for your wealth vision?

  > Investing
  > Accounting
  > Real estate
  > Business
  > Stock market
  > Entrepreneurship

>   Legal entity structuring
>   Retirement planning

- What skills do you need to develop?

>   Accounting
>   Software skills
>   Internet
>   Marketing
>   Sales
>   Investing
>   Project management
>   Leadership

- What resources, teachers and materials are available? Make a list of what you know and what you'll need to research.

Create an expansion plan:

- Select two to three topics, two to three skills and a time frame for learning that is motivating to you, encouraging and challenging.

Track:

- How will you know you've accomplished your goal?
- Find an accountability partner and a time frame for checking in on your growth.

Celebrate!

- As you expand, celebrate your progress and new capacities in a way that feels great for you.

Ed's Story

Ed is fifty-six years old, with three grown children and two grandchildren. After thirty years of working in and consulting with healthcare organizations, he is building a real estate and investment portfolio of his own and creating investment opportunities for others.

I started with small consulting firms that were either my own or in partnership with other individuals. In 1974, when I started out, $17,000 a year was a lot of money. The last year, when I was basically a solo consultant, I billed just a shade under $300,000.

I followed the call into spiritual activity and also had the urge to play out an interest in investing in real estate as a full time activity. At that point, our aggregate net worth was right around one million dollars. After five years, we're approaching five million dollars.

There's a building I bought that's been a great story of the power of giving and receiving. It was a long process to actually buy it because the seller tried to steal the down payment money and not allow the sale to be completed. I wound up having to cause foreclosure on the mortgage and bought it at the foreclosure sale, literally on the courthouse steps. The building was in a neighborhood overrun with drug dealers, prostitutes and pimps. After three-and-a-half years, we were still experiencing a negative cash flow each month in terms of the expenses versus the rent coming in. On the other hand, there were no more pimps, drug dealers or prostitutes in the building! In addition to two retail tenants, there's a sober-living program.

We've been trying to work on how the sober-living program can generate more income so that it can support the building and maybe create a little bit of extra income for the two of us that partnered in this. Yesterday, a friend of a person to whom I offered financial advice met with me. He's been trying to start a high-end addiction program with athletes and movie stars. He was originally referred to me because I fit the profile of a potential investor in his upscale addictions program.

We started talking, and I told him about the building I was working with. Then we discovered I own the building in the neighborhood where he used to buy drugs! He said, "I like doing the ground-level work and really making a difference in the world. Is there some way we can work together that I can bring my talents and skills to help you build your program?" That connection was about more than money.

There's an elementary school a block away from this building. When children get out of school, they can walk by the building without being concerned that they're going to be accosted by people on drugs.

To buy a building and bring it up to habitable standards made a difference. The first time I walked through the building, every faucet and shower was leaking. Once we fixed it, the heating and the water bill was $500 a month less. Today there isn't a leaky faucet, there isn't a leaky pipe, and there's hot water all the time. We spend money, and we're saving money at the same time. None of the tenants have buckets catching water in the bathtubs anymore, so they have a nicer place to live.

We painted the building. We cleaned it up. We put some security wire mesh around the upstairs balcony. We reduced our liability, and we made it a safer place for people to live.

We definitely want to invest so that we're prudent with the money. We're seeking to earn a profit, especially if we bring other investors into our programs. At the same time, we improved the quality of life for the people who live in the building.

Creating wealth is our objective, and we're creating housing for people. We have responsibilities to the sixty families who live there for providing them with a habitable place to live.

That will create income. We'll increase the value of the property. We'll increase the rents that are collected. Making it a better place makes more money, and it becomes an upward spiral of good.

I've always had an underlying belief that one way or another, there would be enough money to do whatever I needed to do in my life. I just always had the confidence when I needed $200 to pay rent, or now when we need $2,000,000 to buy a building. Money is a tool, a tool for getting things done. As my activities have grown and my investment activities have increased, I circulate more money. I bless every transaction that comes in and goes out. I'm conscious about how we manage the flow and feel that we're serving our tenants, our suppliers and our investors.

There have been plenty of times when there were financial struggles. But I knew there was an infinite supply into which I could tap.

It's taken discipline and belief to build our real estate portfolio. We don't have much cash on hand at times. We're putting up $20,000 to $30,000 to secure new deals and then moving forward to figure out how to close. But I'm committed to growing this way. Every time I have to do a loan application, I see that the net worth has gone up since the last time.

I think the most significant idea I work with is that it's not really my money. We're just here to be stewards. We've been given the awesome responsibility of tapping into the infinite flow of the divine and then doing wonderful things with it. From the spiritual point of view, it always shocked me that some spiritual teachings imply that to have money or be wealthy is negative. Once you've been able to take care of your own needs, you're in a position to do things for other people or to do bigger and bigger things in the world that somehow benefit other people.

Actions that are in alignment with the vision we want to reveal, repeated over time with intention, become habits. The best way to create new habits is to choose something and get started, keep going and enjoy the new results.

Many people are familiar with the "21 Day Phenomenon." Dr. Maxwell Maltz was a surgeon who found that the human mind takes about twenty-one days to adjust to a major life change. This twenty-one day period was universally consistent, whether the change was perceived as negative, like a loss of a limb or a loved one, or perceived as positive, like entering into a new romantic relationship. Taking this twenty-one day period into account, the idea for action in this chapter is an encouragement to select a new money meaning habit and do it consistently for twenty-one days.

Will blessing, serving, spiritual giving, managing your money flow and having a wealth expansion plan really get you more money? The only way you'll know is to act.

Chapter Six Review

Questions for Reflection

1) What examples of the *Law of Circulation* have been most inspiring to me? When and where have I gotten back more than I've given in my relationships, work, creativity and community?

2) What, if any, excitement or resistance do I have in blessing, serving, and spiritual giving? What beliefs do I need to empower to get into action?

3) What are the strengths and challenges in my current money management systems?

4) What kind of learning methods work best for me? What forms of education and growth do I enjoy? What helps me thrive?

Ideas for Action

1) 21 Days to Change Program:

- Select one of the habits to get you in the flow of circulating: blessing, serving, spiritual giving, managing the money flow or the wealth expansion plan.

- Choose to do some research, action and reflection every day for twenty-one days to keep the habit alive for you. For example:

- Service. Give loving service at a shelter in your town, do simple anonymous acts of service, and read about or plan for service projects on the other days. Call a friend and let them know what you discovered.

- Spiritual Giving. Calculate a percentage of your income for spiritual giving. Pray and meditate about where to share your spiritual giving on days you're not writing checks.

Tools

Visit **www.themoneykeys.com/tools** to download sample *Financial Foundation Worksheets* for balance sheet, income statement and money flow systems.

Chapter Seven

Your People: Money Models, Mirrors, and Mentors

"You rob no person when you discover your own good. You limit no person when you express a greater degree of livingness. You harm no one by being happy. You steal from no one by being prosperous. You hinder no person's evolution when you consciously enter into the kingdom of your good and possess it today."

– Ernest Holmes

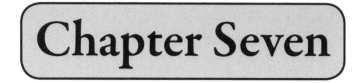

Chapter Seven

Who's in Your Money Game?

Money and its meaning directly or indirectly affect many, if not all, of our relationships and experiences with others. As you deepen your spirituality, strengthen your empowering beliefs and commit to conscious habits around money, you will also become more discerning about whom you're sharing your money life with, including your family, friends, intimates, business partners, vendors, suppliers, investors and network. It matters with whom you're playing in the money game.

The Power of Leverage

When we invest with financial leverage, money's capacity to purchase, create or circulate is increased by borrowing. Banks routinely help people buy $300,000 homes with $30,000 in cash and $270,000 of financial leverage. More leverage means more capacity, more risk and more potential return.

Working, playing, investing, sharing and dreaming with other people about money and its meaning in life is a form of leverage. The more minds, hearts and hands that are involved in your game means the possibility of more results.

Each of us has access to the whole because we are infinite beings, but we don't always express all of it. When we come together, we can accelerate and intensify our collective vibration. We create more. Adding one and one doesn't just result in two, but infinity.

If you are not sharing, learning and connecting with other people but rather hoarding your net worth and hiding your spirituality, the most you can create is the best of your past. Your learning and growing into something new is likely to be just incremental. When you consciously connect with, team up with, work with, play with and pray with others, you become open to new ideas, information and possibilities.

Your People: Past, Present and Future

In this section, first you'll examine who's been influential as models of belief and behavior around money and its meaning. You'll see who's with you now, mirroring back your consciousness and your results in your money life. Then you'll see how you can purposefully choose the people you want to learn from, give to, and play with. You can choose models, mirrors and mentors who support, celebrate and share your vision, your beliefs and your goals.

Models

Our spiritual essence is eternal, intact and untouched by human experience. However, our human bodies, minds and emotional reactions are deeply affected by conditioning. Babies learn the language, culture and habits of their own home, not the homes on another continent. We learn and model words, habits, beliefs and practices we see, feel and hear day after day.

Your family of origin was your first model of inner beliefs and outer behaviors of money. You've already examined the beliefs about money, you, and the world that originated with your family. As an adult, you may be re-acting or acting out behaviors you saw modeled as well. Consciously or unconsciously, you spend or save, share or earn the same way your family did. Or you may be rebelling against the behaviors you saw and doing the opposite.

My parents were a team when it came to household expenses. Mom wrote down, to the penny, the amount of money spent on household items on little slips of paper and tacked them on the bulletin board in the kitchen. Then the slips of paper disappeared as my dad captured the numbers.

Forty years later, I became a late-in-life, first-time wife. I married and began sharing finances for the first time. How did I let my beloved partner know what we spent? I put little post-it notes on the edge of his computer with dollar amounts down to the penny. I became my mother!

Social, Ethnic and Religious Models

Social, cultural, religious and ethnic models of spirituality, beliefs and habits around money affect us as well. The neighborhood or community in which you grew up was filled with examples of individuals and families interacting with one another and with money. You saw literally thousands of models of earning, generating, spending, investing, sharing, borrowing and circulating money. Those patterns and the mental thoughts and emotional energy are part of your consciousness.

In the media, you see people who become wealthy by luck; they won the lottery or gained fame and fortune in ways you envy and want to emulate or in ways you don't respect or understand. Or you see people who have suffered and then are rewarded by winning a prize or being selected for a makeover show.

Money may also mean dominance or excess to some. They may have the idea that the rich spend lavishly and control people, places and beautiful things.

The truth is that these ideas and views are reflections of what you learned over your life. Models from your past are important, whether you're aware of them or not.

You are influenced by what you see and hear constantly. The time, energy and attention you invest in television, movies, magazines, the Internet, hanging out, etc. result in the presentation of new models to you as well. It can be powerful to choose models that are inspiring. 'Choice implies consciousness,' said Eckhart Tolle. Zoning out and unconsciously absorbing anything and everything can have unintended negative effects upon your mental thoughts and emotional energy.

Mirrors

Models are people we have been or are observing. Mirrors are the individuals we actively share our lives with now. With whom are you playing your money game today? Today's people, experiences and circumstances in your money life reflect, or mirror back to you, what you have believed and the choices you have made.

One of the quickest ways of assessing the people who mirror your beliefs and choices in money and meaning is to compile a top ten list:

First, list the ten individuals with whom you spend the most time.

Include your mate, your children, your parents and your siblings if they are close by, as well as your boss, co-workers or partners, your friends, neighbors and community members. Assess each person's consciousness and results when it comes to money.

Create columns with the following headings:

> What reality?
> What game?
> What growth?
> Net worth
> Income

For each column, go down the list of people and capture what you know about that person.

In the "What reality?" column, note whether the person serves a spiritual reality of scarcity, fearing the divine, wholeness, peace, etc. What's the person's dominant spirituality?

In the "What game?" column, decide if each person plays a game of superstition, control, co-creation, freedom, etc.

In the "What growth?" column, capture how each person focuses his or her power in his or her money life. Is it creativity, legacy, competition, survival or thriving?

In the column for net worth, estimate the individual's or family's net worth.

In the income column, capture the person's estimated monthly or yearly income.

The top ten list is not intended to judge others; it's a tool for you to see what's being mirrored back to you by your people. What are the dominant themes of the spirituality of the people around you? What goals are they pursuing? What are their beliefs about competition, winning and losing? What is the average net worth of your team? Average income? You might find the results inspiring, shocking, pleasing or upsetting. It does make a difference with whom you associate!

Now add you to the list. Where do you fit in with the top ten? Are you a leader, replacing number one at the top? Does that work for you? Do you feel that you're creating new possibilities for the people around you? Or do you need friends who are more conscious and more affluent? Are you number eleven, at the bottom and feeling inspired to expand? Are you at the bottom and feeling intimidated? Or are you embarrassed to share the facts? There isn't a right answer; there's only your answer.

Once you've compiled your top ten list, you can make conscious choices about where and with whom you invest your time, energy, attention and resources. It's not about reviewing a credit report before a coffee date or about telling your cousin her consciousness is sub-par. You may find, though, that you are more deliberate and observant as you navigate through family outings, spiritual communities, charitable groups, social causes and neighborhood activities when you desire to match your interests and goals with people who are playing a game that you want to share and join. This is a practice to create conscious partnerships with individuals in your money life where you can inspire, share and support each other powerfully.

Groups

For many people, prosperity partners, mastermind groups and vision teams can be very powerful on their journey through mastery in spirituality, beliefs and habits in their financial lives. When people are accompanied by others who are committed to growth and expansion in their own lives, they are able to see modeled and mirrored around them what's possible in terms of growth, change and expansion. They are able to see different approaches.

A strong group of four to ten people can meet regularly on the phone, in person or over a meal for support, challenge and expansion. I currently belong to three different mastery groups: one for visioning, one for divine feminine beauty and one for wealth-building.

It's great to work and play with a group of people who have mutual respect for ideas, beliefs and values about money and the meaning it has in life. Each individual has his or her own spiritual reality, mental conditioning, financial habits and goals. Together you share a belief that it's possible for you all to be, do and have what you want.

Diversity of strengths and interests is valuable in a mastery group. You learn other processes, agreements and outcomes from each. When you rotate leadership, you all build capacity.

In the tools section at the end of the chapter, you can download the Mastery Group Guidelines. There are tips for creating a group, a protocol for leading weekly telephone meetings, and guidelines for encouraging and challenging each other. Coming together with like-minded and like-hearted people can help you enter into a whole new conversation and a whole new reality about the possibilities of prosperity in your life.

Mental Equivalents

Your people include past models and the current mirrors in your money life, individuals who are with you by choice, by default or by happy accidents. You're also free to consciously choose people to inspire you to develop vivid mental equivalents of the spiritual consciousness, mental and emotional beliefs, and habits you desire to emulate.

Mental equivalent, a term used in the Science of Mind and Spirit philosophy, is the subjective level to which you believe you can be, do or have something. If the invisible, infinite supply of life is like the rushing Niagara Falls, the mental equivalent is the container you use to capture your share of the flow. It's how much you believe you can have. Is it a thimbleful? A bucket? A reservoir?

The mental equivalent is not right or wrong, big or little; it's uniquely yours. To Beverly, living in an abundant universe means her rent is paid by the third of each month, every month. For Jerry, living in an abundant universe means his company is rehabbing three houses this month. For Ellen, living in an abundant universe means giving $3 million to a new foundation dedicated to curing cancer. And for Bob, living in an abundant universe means three years of sobriety and doing an honest day's work for an honest day's pay.

You create the mold into which you pour the infinite supply of the divine. A mental equivalent is putting the "as" in the statement, "It is done unto you *as* you believe." It's like a governor on a car's engine.

A mental equivalent can act like a limit for you. In your financial life, you automatically return to your previous level of experience, unless you do something to change or shift your mental equivalent.

The real estate mogul's father was a very wealthy man. He went to the best schools and lived a very fine life. He was launched into the real estate business through his father's contacts. He accomplished big, creative deals. When a series of deals turned bad and the son faced bankruptcy, his mental equivalent was still there. In his mind, he was still a mogul. Three years later, he rebuilt the real estate portfolio. The mental equivalent of success, creativity and access to contacts and opportunities was established in mental and emotional beliefs and reinforced by the people, models and mirrors surrounding him.

Another example of the power of unconscious mental equivalents is the stories of lottery winners. For many people, winning the lottery is the American dream. For some winners, the lottery can seem more like a nightmare.

Bankrate.com recently published the story of Evelyn Adams, who won the lottery not once but twice, winning a total of $5.4 million. Today, the money has disappeared, and she lives in a trailer. Miss Adams gave money to almost everyone who asked for it. She was caught up in her ability to give money and could not say no. She also had a gambling habit that was intensified by the amount of money she now had to spend. The mistakes she made cost her millions – literally.

Another lottery winner, Ken Proxmire, was a machinist when he won $1 million in the Michigan lottery. He moved to California and went into the car business with his brothers. Within five years he filed for bankruptcy. Ken wanted to take care of everyone, and they all lived the high life for a few years. Now Ken is again working as a machinist.

Without beliefs about yourself, money and its meaning in your life, it's challenging to step into the fact of "winning" money. If you have no models to show you how to behave, manage and live with money, it's hard to suddenly develop those skills.

"For many people, sudden money can cause disaster," says Susan Bradley, a certified financial planner in Palm Beach, Florida, who was interviewed by the Associated Press. She is the founder of the Sudden Money Institute, a resource center for new money recipients and their advisors. "In our culture, there is a widely held belief that money solves problems. People think that if they had more money, their troubles would be over. When a family receives sudden money, they frequently learn that money can cause as many problems as it solves," she says.

Bradley, who authored *Sudden Money: Managing a Financial Windfall,* says winners get into trouble because they fail to address the emotional connection to the windfall. "There are two sides to money. The interior side is the psychology of money and the family relationship to money. The exterior side is the tax codes, the money allocation, etc. The goal is to integrate the two. People who can't integrate their interior relationship with money appropriately are more likely to crash and burn. Often they can keep the money and lose family and friends, or lose the money and keep the family and friends, or even lose the money and lose the family and friends."

Build Your Mental Equivalent

In an abundant and ever-expanding universe, there's always room for growth in your mental equivalents. By cultivating your realization of spiritual principles such as the *Law of Unity*, the *Law of Cause and Effect* and the *Law of Circulation*, you release the false hold of previous limits of mental equivalents.

Expanding your perception of who you are and what you can be and do is a team sport. When you learn from, get inspired by, and commune with other people and their spirituality, beliefs and habits, you grow. You see that something new is possible and come to believe that it's possible for you.

Increasing your mental equivalents through the others with whom you play is a game in which everybody wins. You see what you want expressed by someone else. There's enough to go around. No need for envy. You can say, "That's for me."

Consciously expanding your mental equivalents through modeling other people begins with wanting to expand. It's possible to attract and discover people who serve a God that inspires, play a game that empowers, and pursue goals you admire. It's healthy and inspiring to witness real-life stories of how people earn, save, grow, spend, invest and circulate their money.

Find the people who have some or all of the qualities and results to which you aspire:

- Who are they and what do they do that contributes to their experiences and results?

- What does money mean to them?

- How do they play with others?

- What do they read and study? What do they do with their time?

- What's the quality of their health, their spiritual practice and their relationships?

- What are their beliefs and their behaviors concerning money?

- Is the person a successful artist? Real estate investor? Stay-at-home mom?

The vendors and service providers with whom you work are also part of your money people. Every relationship you have is an opportunity to build a team that is in alignment with your vision, beliefs and choices. Do you want a CPA who's scared or empowered?

Do you need to check the consciousness of your web master? Is your enthusiastic, bright nephew who wants to learn about real estate a potentially great member of your team, even if his educational background is in political science?

You, as a spiritually peaceful, consciously empowered, and behaviorally balanced wealthy person, are a powerful model for the people in your life. It's a spiritual axiom that we get what we give. Your modeling is an example that inspires others to be more connected, free and generous with their money and its meaning. Intend to learn from and teach generous, prosperous, conscious people by being the most expanded individual you can be.

Mentors - Coaches, Experts and Teachers

You have models and mirrors in your money life by default, just by interacting with other people. The category of mentor refers to individuals you deliberately seek out in order that you may learn from and grow with them.

Mentors include coaches, experts and teachers. The learning can be content-focused, such as someone who teaches you about or shows you investment vehicles or meditation techniques. The learning can be process-oriented, such as coaching on how to attract diverse investors for your Internet business or mentoring on developing leadership skills in creating a family partnership for a new venture.

You've probably heard about the leverage of using OPM, other people's money, to invest in real estate, businesses or projects. Working with a teacher, coach or mentor is like OPC, other people's consciousness. You tap into information, ideas and experiences that can help you leverage your efforts.

A coach helps you achieve your goals through helping you develop your beliefs and your habits. The coach is in agreement with you about what you want. He or she then holds you accountable for how you believe, what you are, and what you do in order to achieve the results you say you want. A good coach hears what you say but listens for what you really want. A coach encourages and challenges you to break through resistance or habits that might be in your way.

In conscious wealth-building programs, coaching can be a very powerful way to blend new money practices with new approaches in consciousness. A good coach can be someone who is successful and inspiring to you, but not necessarily an expert in your profession or business. Or he or she can be someone who has the same family background and experiences that you do. You can use the process of spiritual due diligence, which I introduce in this chapter, to help determine if an individual coach is a good fit for you.

Mentoring relationships can be similar to coaching, but often include a shared interest or expertise in a business, professional or spiritual practice. A mentor has been where you'd like to go and is willing to guide, teach and proactively model what you want to be, learn and do. Wealth educator Loral Langemeier recommends forming alliances or joint ventures with individuals and companies as mentors so that you can learn, see and share by doing business together.

Experts and teachers are an important part of a consciously wealthy life. People who are both spiritually and financially wealthy are always committed to learning and growing. Select inspiring teachers and programs that expand you and your knowledge in relevant ways. The spiritual due diligence process is a great way to guide yourself to the best for you.

Selecting Support

To proactively look for mentors, consider the best mix of encouragement and challenge for you. Everyone can benefit from both encouragement and challenge from those with whom we're playing the money game.

Encouragement helps you continue thinking, feeling and doing the things that move you forward. It's positive affirmation. Challenges are supportive experiences that help you stop or change beliefs or behaviors in order to get different results. It's corrective feedback. Encouraging energy feels much like receiving feminine compassion and nurturing. Challenging energy is like a masculine push, a negotiation with your fears to move you into action. Both are valuable.

Simultaneously developing you and your wealth can sometimes be like running a marathon. Twenty years ago, I ran the New York City Marathon. Well, I jogged the New York City Marathon. In a twenty-six mile, four and a half hour long distance race, when you're moving slowly and can see and hear the people from the sidelines, encouraging words and smiles mean a lot.

Sometimes mastering the meaning of money is like interval training with spurts of speed, for which challenge can really help. Although I didn't like it, I increased my overall speed when I was challenged to run short sprints within my daily training runs. It was uncomfortable, but the challenge was worth it. You might see that the resentments you carry toward your ex or business partner still run through your mind. Seeing a counselor may be uncomfortable, but it's time to look at your part in creating the victim-perpetrator dynamic. That's challenge.

The right mix of encouragement and challenge helps you grow. That mix can shift over time. Knowing what you need and when you need it requires a high degree of self-awareness. Your mix is based on your personality, your goals, how you've learned in the past, and what your wealth vision is calling you to be and do.

Spiritual Due Diligence

In money matters, consciousness is everything. Ideally, a teacher, mentor, coach or guide in your wealth journey respects your spirituality, even if you don't share the same beliefs or practices. Choose people based on your commitment to spiritual principles and your desire for money results.

- When you select people to be models, mirrors or mentors, use spiritual due diligence. Discern the inner attributes of people, just as you consider the places and types of deals you choose. You might vet a real estate deal by looking at past deals, the current portfolio, and the skills and assets of the players. You would run the numbers for cash on cash return, appreciation, tax savings, or whatever other criteria were important to you. You can also vet the people and the deal by asking the following questions:

- *What reality are they serving?* Are these people washed up on the desert island of scarcity or are they interested in wholeness?

- *What game are they playing?* Are they imprisoned by their superstitions or are they all about freedom and choice? Would we be co-creating or would we be exploiting and dominating?

- *How are they growing?* Is this all about survival mode or growth? What new knowledge, skills and possibilities would we be building for ourselves and contributing to others?

You have the spiritual, mental, emotion and intuitive resources to be able to answer these questions.

- Gather facts and data so that you can intellectually respond.
- What information about results, structures, policies and information is available?

Close your eyes for a moment and imagine moving forward with this team. Listen to your gut. Are you tense or relaxed? Excited or concerned? Grounded or distracted?

You can also access the wisdom of your body in your spiritual due diligence. Recent studies in the science of kinesiology show that your muscles respond to substances, ideas, people and energy strongly or weakly, depending on whether that idea, person or energy is a strong or weak one for you. Do the following simple self-test with people, projects or deals with whom you are considering playing the money game. **See who and what tests strong or weak for you:**

- Take your left hand and put your thumb and index finger tip together.
- Put your right thumb through the circle formed by the left thumb and index finger, and join your right thumb tip to your right index finger tip. You've formed two interlocking circles.

- You're now able to experience how your body responds to people, ideas and energy by testing how strong or weak your muscles become when you attempt to pull the two circles apart. When you're neutral, most people find there's enough muscle strength to hold both circles intact when you try to move them apart.

- Find your own bodily responses by thinking consciously about and testing people you know are strong or weak for you:

- Select someone who's been a strong supporter of your spiritual vision and your prosperity. Think about that individual and feel, as you pull your fingers against each other, that you have the strength to hold them together. Release your hands and shake them out.

- Select a person who you know is uninspiring to you or who you know is not a supporter of your vision or choices. Perhaps that person's scarcity fears or superstitions get in the way. Think about that individual and feel, as you pull your fingers against each other, that even if you want to, you can't hold them together.

That's your individual baseline. Some may find this kind of approach a bit outside of the norm, but I know it's worked for me! It's a practice to immediately tap into the sometimes wordless wisdom that is there within us all. You conduct your spiritual due diligence with your intellect, your intuition and your physical wisdom.

A Team You Can Trust

Developing a sense of trust in the confidence and judgment of those with whom you play the money game is essential. Building an effective team of spiritual and practical support and collaboration is an adventure. There may be losses you experience when people who have been very involved in your life become less prominent. Changing is not always comfortable or easy, nor is your change always easy for those around you.

Take a moment and think about where you were five years ago.

- Who were you romantically involved with?
- Where were you living?
- What did you wear?
- What did you eat?
- Who did you associate with?
- What hobbies were you engaged in?
- How much money did you have?
- What were the greatest desires of your heart?
- What job or profession or creative activities were you involved in?

Now come back to today. For most people, over a period of five years not everything remains the same. We grow and change.

Author and consultant William Bridges is known for describing change as a form of transition. In transitions, there are endings, a neutral zone and new beginnings. When you initiate a new spiritual vision for your life and money, there may be relationships or activities that end. Bridges encourages us to honor the grief of endings.

It may take time to create the game you want to play and attract the people you want to play with, or there may be challenges. There can be a sense of inertia or uncertainty, like a neutral zone.

In the neutral zone you balance patience and persistence. Coaches, teachers and guides help guide you toward relationships, beliefs and habits that honor where you've been and move you towards where you're going.

Excitement emerges in the transition phase of new beginnings. Creativity is strong, and new projects and people show up. Understanding this idea of transitions helps you manage yourself and those around you with compassion and skill.

Infinite Possibility

It is spiritually uplifting to see models of people serving a reality of wholeness, choosing to play a game of freedom, and thriving through growth and expansion.

In 1975, Bill Gates, along with partner Paul Allen, started Microsoft. Though the company was worth very little at the beginning, within a few years Microsoft had several products and a reputation for shrewd business deals. Today, over 80% of all PCs use Microsoft software and operating systems. In 2006, the company had sales of $46.1 billion. Microsoft now does business in every country in the world, and Bill Gates has personally amassed a fortune in excess of $30 billion based on his shares of Microsoft alone, not including his other holdings. In addition to Microsoft being one of the fastest growing companies of all time, Bill Gates's story is also about unprecedented giving. In 2000, Bill and his wife Melinda created the Bill and Melinda Gates Foundation. To date, the foundation has given more that $13.5 billion to charities around the world, most of which involve children and education.

While the Gates family is an extreme example of what is possible, you might also be surprised to know that your neighbor or the janitor in your apartment building is also generating and sharing wealth.

The Associated Press recently published an interesting story about the possibility of saving, giving and making a difference that might expand your idea of what's possible.

In Saint Leo, Florida, Evelyn V. Burns, a member of the Seminole tribe, left Saint Leo University $350,000 in her will, the university's largest bequest in its history. Burns, a retired executive assistant for an investment manager, was 87 when she died. She never married, had no family still living, and lived alone. For as long as they had known her, friends said Miss Burns was quiet about her private life and gave no indication she had amassed approximately $1.5 million in savings.

University spokeswoman, Jenifer LeBeau, said no one at the school remembered her being involved with Saint Leo, except to note that she had started donating gifts to the school in the 1960s. What inspired the giving? We may not know for sure, but we can be certain that Evelyn V. Burns created more opportunity through her giving.

Reggie's Story

Reggie is a handsome, charming, African-American man who looks younger than you'd think for a great-grandfather. He's passionate about the discipline of mind and the importance of models in playing an expanded money game.

I came from a very humble but good-hearted environment. My dad died when I was fourteen years old. I didn't know too much about him. He and my mom had separated.

One of my first imprints of my dad happened one fall. It was around the Jewish holidays. You couldn't get anything from the store at times, and sometimes between paydays there wasn't much food in the house. I remember one day when I was a little boy my grandmother and my aunt had gone out to try to get some bread and eggs or something. It was dark, and I was hungry. I knew where there was a stash of uncooked raw macaroni. I remember going into the kitchen and some of it had spilled under a cabinet. I was reaching under this cabinet and eating these raw macaronis. I looked over my shoulder and my dad was looking at me, and he said, "We'll have something soon, son. But I can see you're a survivor."

I grew up in an environment that, for all practical purposes, was impoverished. But I didn't have an impoverished life. My mother raised me by herself. We had a one-room apartment. I slept on the sofa in the kitchen until I was eighteen years old. I went into the military at eighteen, came back, and got my own apartment.

At least half the people in the community were on public assistance. I saw those that did have jobs go to work and come home dirty. Every now and then, a hero in the neighborhood was somebody that would get a new car, and everybody would gather around. This was a big thing. The drug dealers all seemed to have the nicest cars, but they would wind up dead or in prison before too long. I knew that I wanted something more in life.

When I was growing up, people said to me, "You don't pay attention long enough to do anything very academically challenging, and you don't seem to know which damn side of the hammer to use, so we don't know what you're going to do."

They had no clue that I'm entrepreneurial. I'm creative. Let me sell something! I got a paper route, and I started hustling money. I started doing some other things, some things we won't talk about. They might still be looking for me.

When I came out of the military, I went to work for a utility company. My mother said, "Go get some work. You're strong, get some work!" They had me sweeping floors and cleaning washrooms. I said, "This is the pits. I'm greater than this."

"It's honest work, son."

"Yeah, I know, but it can be more honest with somebody else! It's dishonest to me. I'm not cleaning no damn toilets."

Shortly afterward I discovered commissioned sales.

*I wanted something different, and I found the world of commissioned sales and personal growth. I got a hold of **Think and Grow Rich.** I read this book and expanded my mind and my vibration. I had a spirit of expectancy. I started to hang out with people who were reading books and listening to tapes about positive thinking and sales success. I would talk to people, and they would buy things that they wanted. I would talk to more people, and they would buy what they wanted. And I would talk to more people, and they would buy what they wanted.*

But since I had been conditioned to working five days a week for $250, I would work three days a week making $500 and take the rest of the time off. I'd go backward because I was just sitting around drinking beer and spending the money. I went from a very prosperous attitude into default. I was just trying to get by. I was conditioned to simply getting by. I came out west in 1978 for the first time. I was pursuing my dreams in a commissioned sales job. I was constantly looking in the classified ads for another opportunity to change my life. I saw one. They flew me out. I saw Rolls Royces, gated communities, and homes with fountains. That blew my mind.

I came from the projects. I said, "I ain't never going back." Unfortunately, the law didn't like the way the company that I was affiliated with did things and shut it down. So I had to go back out into the cold.

I swore I wasn't coming back. There's a saying that nothing can defeat a made-up mind.

My greatest win to date was when I came out west again. With $2,000 of my own and $2,000 from my family, I started a limousine service. I bought a used limousine and drove it on the weekends.

I had been piddling around with real estate. A friend of mine got me a job as a loan officer with a legitimate company, a bank. I wrote loans for real estate. I got pretty good at it and helped people, first time homebuyers. They were folks that didn't have many places to turn to, particularly in the minority communities where the bank had policies that made it difficult for them to borrow money.

The federal government had stepped in and called the bank on their policies by holding up a merger it had planned. The folks at the bank hired me out of the community because I had been active with some of the interest groups and had a little bit of a real estate background. So they trained me to go into the African-American, Native American and Hispanic communities and write loans so they could do the merger.

I had about $10 million to loan. They almost gave me carte blanche. *It took me about a half an hour to get rid of it! I gave money to everybody. Finally, after they met their quota, they fired my ass. And I said, "I've got a limousine. I'm going to drive my limousine." And I drove that limousine to a $250,000 annual income. I went from the streets to the suites!*

*With some challenges in real estate and a period of losing my focus, I'm working my way back up from a version of the streets. I'm on my way back to the suites. I learned once how to do it. I can do it again. I hear the positive messages from my teachers who wrote the books like **Think and Grow Rich** over and over again in my mind.*

I can feel the early modeling of the survival modality still with me today. I was not taught how to tap into the infinite abundance, which is energy that exists all around us.

I distinctly remember moving out west again in 1987 and meeting a gentleman from my hometown. He said, "So what brought you out here?" And I said, "Man! I came out here to get rich. There is nothing but opportunity out here." I had the visions of grandeur because the east was cold, it was conservative, and it was old money. This was an entrepreneurial hotbed. I distinctly remember he said, "Man, these folks ain't gonna let you get rich." That is a psychology that prevails, and I know that it's conditioned.

I have recognized that my people, for the most part, are suffering from the disease of disharmony, a disconnection to their higher being, which is infinite, abundant and inexhaustible. But they don't know that because they have been taught otherwise. We were taught to simply suffer and survive until we get to another reality when we leave this earthly plane. But I can look around at the world, and I can say, "Well, these people are in poverty, and these people are in abundance, and that has nothing to do in my opinion with the availability or the lack of availability of money."

I was so determined that I wound up out west. Now I'm living in a house that I could have only dreamed about. I came out of a one-room apartment where I slept in the kitchen on the couch. I know that anything is possible, but I must maintain my belief. The family, friends and business relationships I choose today are built on shared values and goals and reflect my deep love for where I've been and my certainty that more is possible!

Money is energy. It is life. It expands who you are, and it also makes you more of who you are. I've heard that if you're a louse, you'll be more of a louse, and if you're a wonderful, magnificent person, you'll be more of a wonderful, magnificent person. What I know beyond a shadow of a doubt is that I am truly free.

Chapter Seven Review

Questions for Reflection

1) Who have been the most vivid models of beliefs and behavior around money in my family life?

2) Who are the social, political, economic or media models of behavior concerning money to whom I currently pay attention?

3) What mix of support, including encouragement and challenge, serves me best right now? What groups, prosperity partners, coaches, mentors and teachers am I drawn to?

Ideas for Action

1) **Do the Top Ten List:**

- Write down the names of ten people with whom you invest the most time and energy right now.

- Select the areas of mirroring you want to examine, such as spiritual reality, money game, money habits, net worth or income.

- For each category and for each person, capture the key piece of data.

- Look at the columns to see the themes or the numerical averages for net worth or income.

- Look at how you rank within the columns.

- Look at the rows to get a sense of how that individual is showing up in your life.

- What insights emerge about you, your beliefs and your choices? Are there things to say or actions to take?

2) **Conduct Spiritual Due Diligence:**

- Select a project, vendor, client, group or program about which you want to make a holistic decision concerning your current and future participation.

Ask:

- *What reality are we serving?* Are these people washed up on the desert island of scarcity or are they interested in wholeness?

- *What games are we playing?* Are the people with whom I'd be working imprisoned by their superstitions or are they all about freedom and choice? Would we be co-creating or would we be exploiting and dominating?

- *How are we growing?* Is this all about survival mode or growth? What new knowledge, skills, and possibilities would we be building for ourselves and contributing to others?

3) **Develop your Mental Equivalents:**
- Review your qualitative and quantitative wealth goals.

- Select at least one of each to examine if an expanded Mental Equivalent could inspire you:

- Can you meditate more regularly like _____?
- Could your net worth grow by _____?
- What's possible for others that could be possible for you?

Tools

Visit **www.themoneykeys.com/tools** to download *Mastery Group Guidelines.*

Chapter Eight

Your Partner: Sharing Love and Money

"...as we let our own light shine, we unconsciously give other people permission to do the same. As we're liberated from our own fear, our presence automatically liberates others."

– Marianne Williamson

Chapter Eight

How Money and People Work Together

Money is a tool for expressing how the natural, eternal, infinite intelligence of your creative source flows in your relationships. Living is circulation. Whether you're a single person who is self-employed, part of a large family business, or involved in multiple partnerships, you give and receive with people.

Money and Conflict

Why is money at the heart of so much conflict in intimate relationships? It's because of what you make it mean. In a romantic, intimate partnership, money can mean safety, love, control or identity.

If getting money from someone means you'll be safe, then you're threatened when that person doesn't think, feel and do what you want them to concerning money. If another person's beliefs and behavior with money are supposed to show how they love you, then your connection to love seems to be at the mercy of money. If you equate your identity with a certain amount of money or a particular lifestyle provided by someone else, your very life feels threatened if it is taken away. If you feel that you're responsible for another's financial well-being along with your own, that person's needs and spending make you feel resentful and depleted. The traps of scarcity, superstition and survival mode cause particular suffering in relationships.

One way people try to solve this dilemma is to blame the money. They say that money shouldn't be so important in relationships or community. It's not money that is the "root of all evil." It is the "love of money," the worship of the symbol, the mistaken idea that something other than the divine is our source.

The trouble isn't the money. Money is neutral, just a symbol or potential energy. When you make the symbol mean more than life, love, worth, value, justice, peace, compassion or unity, you are in the hell of your consciousness. You feel separate from the divine. The solution is always a return to serving wholeness, choosing co-creation and acting consciously with your money. You can use money to celebrate your true, limitless value and the inherent value of your mate, your family, your friends, your neighbors and the world.

This chapter includes the ideas of healing your individual past and of coming together consciously to determine the form and focus of your partnership. You'll also find ideas for passion and some practical tips for communication and common goals. You and your mate can develop spirituality, beliefs and habits in a money map together.

First, and Always, the Self

Your individual financial beliefs and behaviors are where you can make the biggest impact on shifting the quality of your intimate relationships. Katherine Woodward Thomas, author of *Calling in "The One:" Seven Weeks to Attract the Love of your Life,* reminds us that, "When we change our relationship with ourselves, our external world changes accordingly."

Start with the self. If you have consumer debts, a gambling addiction, a painful experience from the past, a spending problem, or any other kind of real issue or challenge you need to deal with, first get the support you need to heal the past. Tell the truth to a loving and supportive coach, counselor, or advisor. Make reparations to yourself for being out of alignment with what is true about you. At heart, each person is innocent, loving, free, prosperous and good. Get the encouragement and challenge you need to build empowering beliefs about yourself and change your behaviors. Make whatever reparations or amends you need to make in order to share from a place of spiritual strength.

This does not mean that if you have credit card debt, a bankruptcy, alimony payments or other financial challenges that you cannot create a loving, prosperous and adult relationship. It does mean that you need to have a spiritual context for addressing those things as you build a relationship with someone. Get your own money consciousness in alignment with wholeness, and you'll attract or inspire wholeness in the people around you. Get into a money game of co-creation, and you'll be met by companions at the same vibration. Circulate the flow as you bless, serve and give, and you'll be surrounded by people interested in doing the same things. You have to become what you want to see in your current partner or a new one.

Heal the Past

The past has no hold over you, except the hold you give it. Nothing that happened to you or that you did can diminish that precious, spiritual part of you. In your intimate partnerships, you can be free no matter what your current mate or ex is doing or not doing. You can be prosperous, no matter what your net worth is today because you operate with spiritual qualities which are always infinite, eternal, creative and giving.

You may carry disappointments, resentments, guilt or incompletion from the past with exes, stepfamily, children, siblings or parents. You may harbor hurt from problems around wills, bankruptcy, alimony, debts, gambling, betrayals and spending. If those situations are still active in your thoughts and feelings, there will be an impact on your current intimate partnership. Healing the incompletion includes:

Setting the intention to heal:
Make the decision that you want to be released from this situation.

In your prayers or meditation, ask for spiritual guidance and support in healing.

Confessing what happened:
Write out or talk out the whole story to a trusted friend, prosperity partner or counselor.

Include what happened, the meaning you created out of it, and how you're affected today.

Release any emotions you need to with tears, yelling, and so forth.

Burn the paper you've written. Shred the documents. Give away the mementos.

Choosing to forgive:
Consciously release the judgments about yourself and all those involved.

Choose to see yourself and everyone else as spiritually whole and one with the higher power.

Getting the lesson:

What did you learn, discover, reveal or gain from this experience that you can bring into your own life and your current intimate partnership?

Capture your gift or lesson. You earned it! Do something wonderful for yourself as a celebration of your freedom!

In a spiritually mature approach to love and money, you realize there are no victims and no perpetrators. Take responsibility now to be, do and have what you want.

In creating current-day prosperous partnerships, forgiveness becomes an ongoing practice. An important aspect of healthy forgiveness in a relationship includes having and keeping good boundaries. Continue to stay mentally and emotionally current with your partner around your money lives.

It's Your Partnership

All of these ideas about intimate partnerships apply to people who are married, people who are living together, whether they are heterosexual or homosexual, family partnerships and business partners. The form of relationship you choose reflects the spirituality, the mental and emotional beliefs, and the habits you choose.

Marriage is a convention to which we give meaning. It is a legal agreement and a social construct. We are the ones who make marriage mean something through our beliefs, attitudes, opinions and behaviors. Be willing to create your own meaning out of what is of the highest integrity and spiritual value to you so your marriage can have the meaning that you create and decide for it.

One disabling belief is that marriage automatically brings safety and security. It is like believing that money will keep you safe when it cannot, that the government will keep you safe, or that your house, guns, locks, family pedigree, college education or credit cards will provide you safety. None of those things are going to keep you safe. Your true safety, security, peace of mind and well-being come from your connection to the infinite eternal nature of life. If you believe your good comes from an external symbol of any kind, then you are amiss, even if that external symbol is marriage or something like it.

One of the most painful things I have seen as a spiritual counselor and teacher is the dismay, resentment, anger and victimization created around marriage. Some are disappointed with how marriage has been, and some have the sense that either being married or not being married limits the opportunity to express, to live and to thrive. You decide what marriage means to you.

Yours, Mine and Ours

If you feel the reality of the *Law of Unity*, you see that the human conventions of boundaries, property lines and bank accounts are really out of touch with the truth. Everything in a flowing, infinite united universe belongs to us all.

Indigenous peoples in many traditions hold the idea that you cannot own a piece of the sky or the earth. That might seem silly or naïve to contemporary Western culture. But what if there is a deeper truth about ownership? Can we really own a piece of what is indivisible?

In our world and our economic constructs today, it's efficient to make distinctions between your having this plot of land and our having that business enterprise. Your partner came into the marriage with certain assets and you have responsibilities to your children. You might benefit from keeping things distinct. How do you balance your unity and your individuality? In a conscious spiritual partnership around money, one of the great questions to contemplate and answer together is "What is yours, mine and ours?"

Value Your Differences

There are two kinds of energies of creation. There is pursuit energy, and there is attraction energy. Both are valuable, and each has its place.

Pursuit energy is more masculine; it is purposeful, directional energy. In a spiritual practice there is definitely a place for that energy. Pursuit energy has you looking for evidence that there is more than enough to go around. It has you learning and accessing people, teachers, material, music and CD's that support that idea.

Attraction energy is more feminine. It is a receptive, opening and a desiring of something without necessarily pursuing it, except from a spiritual point of view. In an attraction approach you open yourself to inspiration through journaling, reflective meditation, or opening the heart and the body energy to the spiritual idea.

We all have masculine and feminine energy within us. Understand your individual strengths and where you need to grow. Then become comfortable and confident in sharing those with your partner so that you can contribute the values that you have to each other. You can create goals together that also bring out the best in you.

The Power of Communication

Frank Pankow has dedicated almost twenty years to serving a wide variety of clients and professionals through his firm, which specializes in the valuation of closely-held operating companies, family-controlled entities and professional practices. He's sensitive to the importance of providing excellent advice as well as quality technical valuations to clients. "I help people on the second worst days of their lives," he says. Those days can involve the dissolution of marriages, businesses and estates due to death, divorce, bankruptcy, litigation and other challenges for which the division of assets requires professional advice and expertise.

I asked Frank to comment on the biggest challenges individuals face in their intimate and business financial partnerships and specific strategies to create prosperous, satisfying, positive partnerships.

"I would say that the plus in a relationship as it revolves around money is sharing information. All too often in my practice, I see one of the spouses or significant others taking the leadership role or the sole role of handling all the finances. That's a big mistake. If only one spouse is dealing with the intricacies of the family finances, then the other spouse is ignorant to what's going on, so it's almost impossible under that scenario for the spouses to have a common goal or understanding.

Often one spouse will handle all the finances and the other spouse will delegate all of those responsibilities to that person only because he or she doesn't like doing it, is not good at it or not interested in it. But then, when something negative happens, such as the death of the financial spouse or divorce, the non-financial spouse is completely in the dark. He or she finds him- or herself at a loss at to what the family finances are, what their level of income is, what the taxes are on that income, and so on. This creates sheer terror in the non-finance spouse's mind.

    The lack of common goals is not the only problem. Without communication, you also have more resentment and misunderstanding. Take the example of a traditional nuclear family. Let's say the husband in this scenario will handle all the finances and the wife is completely ignorant of the finances – I see this a great deal. Sometimes the wife will go out and spend freely because she has no concept of what the income, taxes and other expenses of the family unit are. This creates a lot of ill will and stress on the part of the spouse responsible for finances. I also see numerous businesses in which a woman is the entrepreneur or financial partner, and the man is free spending and unengaged.

    If both parties don't have the same financial goals, then they will not be able to focus in on the finances that are required to achieve those goals. For example, if both parties want to retire early, perhaps when they're fifty years old, and one spouse keeps the other in the dark about the finances, then the one that's in the dark may freely spend all the money that's needed to reach that common goal.

    For couples who do want to create a partnership, the most important aspect is sharing information. While both spouses need not be equally interested in the finances of the family, they need to at least sit down once a month and go over what the income is and how the money is being spent and evaluate if that money is really meeting their goals.

    The establishment of goals is a good first step for many couples. For example, if there are big-ticket items each of them wants, they must come to agreement on priorities and understand the finite income they have. If one spouse wants a $10,000 diamond ring and the other spouse wants an $80,000 sports car, then they need to reconcile how they're going to achieve those goals, as one may be diametrically opposed to the other. This can create a great deal of conflict in the relationship.

Common goals can also be things such as how to finance retirement plans. Younger people for whom buying a first home is a huge investment may choose to focus on how they will get the down payment for a starter home.

If you and your spouse have different family patterns or histories about money, strong communication is helpful. We see instances on a regular basis where one spouse comes from a very spoiled or pampered background and now expects their spouse to provide that same type of pampering and luxury. The only way to get past those ingrained ideas and expectations is to sit down and decide what they are trying to achieve financially. Couples need to raise issues like, "What college do we want our children to go to?" "Where do we want to live at certain stages in our relationship?" That's proactive as opposed to asking the question, "Where are we going to get the money to pay this Visa bill?"

Shared information, goals and decision-making forms the basis for a shared sense of what's so, what's possible and who we need to be spiritually, mentally, emotionally and practically."

Create a Money Partnership

The universal principles and practices in *The Money Keys* can be practiced individually or together. Use the audio or written guidelines to see what's so and what's possible for you as a couple. See where you can develop your shared spirituality, strengthen your shared beliefs, and create joint money habits.

Another practice for couples is the *Couples Love & Money Checklist,* which will show you how to share information, create goals and understand each other's expectations and roles concerning money.

The Money Keys Practice:
Couples Love & Money Checklist

Wealth vision
The uplifting spiritual idea of wealth in our relationship (see visioning in chapter four.)

What's so:
Financial assets, liabilities and responsibilities from the past
Current net worth, income, financial facts

What's possible:
Goals: six months, one year, five years
Spiritual qualities
Projects/gifts/dreams

Spirituality: **What reality are we serving?**
- Our shared spiritual practices
- How we want to grow spirituallyz

Beliefs: **What game are we playing?**
- What's a win for us as a couple in terms of projects, people and ideas?
- What beliefs are we empowering?

> ## *Habits:* How are we growing together?
> - What money tasks can we bless together?
> - Where can we serve together?
> - What spiritual giving are we doing?
> - What's the flow of our money management?
> - Percentage of income to giving, investing, play and expenses.
> - Spending agreements: dollar amounts for individual/joint decisions, who handles the bills, and other financial agreements.
> - Wills, trusts, insurance, legal issues and goals.
> - Accounting, software, mechanics of money management.
> - Our expansion plan: What financial, spiritual or educational growth will support us?

What About Passion?

What about prosperity and passion? Can those things go together?

David Deida, author of *Intimate Communion*, describes how a polarity arises from the healthy interplay of masculine and feminine energy and attraction of opposites, either between a man and a woman or between people of the same sex. Masculine energy is the energy of direction and purpose. Feminine energy is the energy of embodiment and manifestation. The masculine strives for freedom. The feminine longs for love. These energies interact very powerfully to create passion and creativity in our lives.

When it comes to an adult romance and the management of money, the roles you choose to play are driven by the meaning you give them. A passionately sexual, romantic relationship requires two adult people who feel empowered to express passion from a sense of self-worth. If you feel that you have to exchange your sexuality for money, or that your worth just comes from the money you provide, it can be hard for you to express yourself fully in romance and passion. If you feel anxious and of no value in your financial life, it can be challenging to feel truly worthy and deserving in other areas, including romance!

The goal is to have your choices, goals and roles in your financial partnership support the interplay of passion and romance that works for you.

Julia's Story

Julia remembers her childhood in a small New York City apartment with three generations of women.

Mom would tell the story of when my dad died when I was nine years old. She didn't know where money for bread and milk would come from. We shopped at Sears and Macy's, but I really preferred Saks and Lord & Taylor. It angered me that some people walking down Fifth Avenue could spend anything they wanted and we couldn't. Mom would always say, "Those women have husbands who support them." So marrying rich was high on my list of ways to get designer clothes and a prosperous life.

I married a man whose parents were multi-millionaires. They had a seat on the New York Stock Exchange. Our fourth date was a long weekend at the Grand Lucaya in the Bahamas. Our wedding was on Park Avenue, and the reception was at the Twenty-One Club in Manhattan. My ring was from Tiffany's, and our honeymoon was a month in Europe. At twenty-five years old I moved into our just-built California atrium ranch house on a couple of pine-covered acres on a golf course in New Jersey.

The Wall Street stockbroker husband turned out to be a scam artist and a functional alcoholic. Despite the extreme luxury, for the most part, the whole scenario felt horrible. We divorced. I was worn down with the legal battles and lost custody of my children. I eventually went to live in ashrams to try to rebuild my sense of sanity and understand what kind of world could possibly allow this to happen.

I became a disciple of an Indian tantric master and lived in a commune. I saw rich people, poor people, pretty people and plain people who all had issues. The people who liked making money and were good at it did that. The people who had other talents did what they did best and were supported by the people who liked making money. It made a lot of sense to me. It was intelligent and cooperative. Seeing that another way was possible helped me heal. I found my center and moved back into modern society, but I kept my spiritual center strong.

Today I'm living somewhere in between the mansion and the ashram. I allow money to flow to me easily, naturally and abundantly. I feel free to share it. And I'd rather not have to pay too much attention to it. It serves me, I don't serve it. It flows to me like a clear, clean, warm, bubbling stream, effortlessly and eternally. Money is a barometer of our evolution as a species, and about as clumsy a communication tool as we can get, but I have hope! I want the natural abundance that exists on this planet to be made available to ALL people through responsible circulating and sharing.

I know that having more or less money will not make me happy or unhappy. But I also know that I must do my part to let money serve my self-care and support me in giving my gifts to the world. I've come to respect money, not fear it or worship it. When I think about creating an intimate partnership around money from where I am now, I know that I must hold my own inner worth very highly. I made the mistake once of over-valuing the outer symbols of money, and I won't do that again.

221

Women and Money

Julia's story is useful for all the women who can relate to the socially reinforced idea that money is controlled by men. Women who really want to live from wholeness must reclaim a sense of choice when it comes to money.

Women can celebrate and empower female friends, daughters, sisters, mothers and partners by providing accurate information and emotional encouragement as well as financial support. Women can challenge the cultural ideas about women and money that are insane, ridiculous and downright wrong.

An otherwise good book I read about how women must care for themselves to create romantic, respectful marriages suggested that women hand over all the finances to their husbands. This author proposed that handling money is inherently too stressful, complicated and hard for women. Not only is this factually untrue, it's a disabling idea!

My favorite women's magazine had an issue dedicated to mastery. Leading-edge experts gave interesting advice on nutrition, skincare, relationships and self-esteem. But the financial experts seemed to be caught in a worldview from a century ago. The investment advisors suggested that boring investments were the best because reliability was the most a woman should hope for. Another suggested that women make decisions in their twenties and stick to them throughout their lives, assuming that women's jobs, needs and decisions don't change. And finally, women should just do everything they can to prevent bad things from happening. I'm exaggerating just a bit, but the level of sophistication and empowerment of other content in the issue was much higher than in the money conversation.

Would anyone suggest that women turn over their communication, their food and their health care to men because it's just too hard, complicated or scary? I hope not! If you choose it, it's incredibly wonderful to be taken care of and provided for by a loving partner. It is fabulous for a woman to feel the generosity of her provider as he (or she) takes care of the family. It's awesome to have a great team to do your accounting and investing, but not because you're incapable of taking care of yourself!

It is vital for men to know they have the power to contribute, create, provide and protect, whether they are staying home with children, creating art, or working more traditional jobs to bring home the bacon. It is equally vital for women to know they are at one with an infinite, generous, loving universe. Women have a tremendous capacity for contribution, for creating flows of income simply through their own being. Women need to know that it is possible to develop skills and capacities to invest, work, create, give and receive supply, whether they are staying home with the children or running a huge corporation.

We Are Already Wealthy

My beloved Bill and I first began our journey of developing a greater sense of wealthy living after we'd been married about a year and a half. We already had a friendly, functional approach to our finances, but it was becoming clear that something greater was possible. What could it be like to live a wealthy and prosperous life? What would we be creating if we kept thinking, feeling and doing what we had been? We started a process of financial education, launched a new business, and invested in real estate, all guided by a vision statement that emerged from our joint visioning sessions.

Our Wealth Vision: We are already wealthy. We consciously choose a life of abundance, passion and creativity. Our ideas and activities generate prosperity and joy and, therefore, serve all. In our loving partnership, cash flows, assets grow and there's plenty of time and energy for everything.

Each word is carefully chosen. When we ask, "What's the money for?" we have our answer. Money is a tool for us to live an inspired life.

We also chose a visual image that captures the essence of wealth for us: a quiet wooden bench overlooking the Big Sur coastline on the California coast. We met at a retreat center called Esalen in Big Sur, California, where the mountains meet the sea. The beautiful coastline, hilly mountains, green grass, dark trees, blue water and craggy rocks really are, to us, the epitome of the statement, "We are already wealthy."

In addition to the vision, we also have shared goals. We have a sense of the net worth and level of passive and active income we want to have, and what kinds of work we want to do individually and together. We have defined prosperity as a number of dollars earning a certain return and a quality of life of physical health, spiritual practice, family, romance and fun.

We also have formal and informal agreements for making decisions about investments and giving. Our money management habits build on our skills and our strengths. Having both individual and joint fun money accounts has been a great strategy.

Recently Bill bought yet another bicycle. I believe it cost more than I could ever conceive of paying for a bike, but I don't really know what it cost. And I don't care to know! It's none of my business. It's his business. It's his fun money. He can spend it on whatever he likes.

I recently bought a series of eight deep-tissue massages for the price of seven at an upscale spa. Does Bill need to know how much that cost? No way. He might start thinking about all the bicycling gear he could get with that much money.

The massages make me happy. The bicycle makes him happy. The freedom and respect make us both happy. That's a good investment!

Chapter Eight Review

Questions for Reflection

1) How have scarcity, superstition, and survival mode played a part in past relationship challenges about money and its meaning? What insights do I have about myself based on the past?

2) What form of intimate relationship around money would really be right for me/us?

3) What are the individual strengths and skills that my partner and I bring to our spiritual and financial relationship?

4) What are the individual areas I need to heal to co-create the prosperous partnership I desire?

Ideas for Action

1) Vision together:

- With your partner, engage in the visioning process by yourselves or with a group on a regular basis.
- Use the audio or written process as a guide.
- Commit to capturing the qualities, images and ideas from visioning and incorporating that wisdom into your spiritual and financial practices.

2.) Make agreements:

- Together, create, capture and commit to specific financial agreements about your money and every aspect of its circulation that is important to you.

- Determine how you'll keep your agreements.

3) Share your Passions!

- Find a fun way to celebrate your prosperity and your partnership.

- Choose a service project, a pampering experience or giving a great gift.

- You are already wealthy. Enjoy!

Tools

Visit **www.themoneykeys.com/tools** to download the *Couples Love & Money Checklist.*

Chapter Nine

Your World: What the Money's Really For

"There is a tremendous strength that is growing in the world through sharing together, praying together, suffering together and working together."

– Mother Theresa

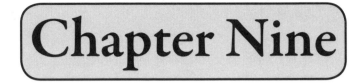

Chapter Nine

Sharing Ownership

I own six percent of an apartment building in a small Texas town. Eight of us, including several first time real estate investors, share ownership of the property. We also share an ethical and spiritual agreement that our ownership is creating a positive contribution for everyone.

When our management team first looked at the building, we started from the idea that there could be a win in this game for the seller, our buying group, the tenants, the town, everybody. We offered a fair price with some creative financing, and the family who owned the building was happy to move on.

Our team met with the on-site property manager and the bookkeeper. Our team shared the details of cash flow and maintenance costs. We offered a bonus for keeping costs down, which involved them and gained their support. We repaired the driveway and several units. Tenants loved what we did. The number of slow-paying renters went down. The vacancy rate dropped from twelve percent to three percent in the first quarter. Our investor group enjoyed even better returns than our original projections. Everybody won. The money in this deal was for creating affordable, quality housing through a well-managed investment, and also for serving the wholeness and dignity of all.

You and the World

This book focuses on individuals who are already committed to mastery of the self and wealth. It's about creating your money map, which really is everyone's money map. Who you are in life makes a difference because you're at one with all of life. The meaning you choose to make contributes to the world because the spirituality you cultivate, the beliefs you strengthen, and the actions you take make a difference.

Dissolving "Rich Are Greedy" and "Poor are Needy"

Everyone has been affected by the cultural attitudes of contemporary society. One set of cultural beliefs that is both common and particularly insidious is that the rich are greedy and should be resented, and the poor are needy and should be pitied. These ideas are reinforced in the media in classical favorites such as Charles Dickens' *A Christmas Carol* and in current television makeover shows.

For all the attention and energy our society places on fairness, we still live in a stratified society. Studies show that Americans' ability to rise above, or fall below, their parents' economic class is the same as thirty-five years ago. Many blame the ills of society on the rich having too much or the poor not having enough.

So what makes you decide which class you fall into? Are you conditioned to be in the same class as your parents and grandparents, no matter what your financial situation is? Labels and class distinctions aren't necessarily based on fact or on a dollar figure. They are based on perceptions. If you cultivate your spirituality, strengthen empowering beliefs, and take on conscious money habits, you build capacity to break out of any limited ideas of class, past history or future possibilities. How do you take an expansive view and inspire, encourage and support others to find their vision of a wealthy, prosperous life, regardless of their financial circumstances?

If you really want to create and sustain a positive, prosperous, powerful life for all, you must dissolve any lingering sense of the ideas that the rich are greedy and the poor are needy. One of the most powerful ways to build new belief is to gather evidence for a new idea. If you think rich people are greedy, that is what you will find. Beliefs attract evidence. What if rich people aren't greedy? What if greedy people are greedy? Greed is one of the ways the money trap of scarcity gets expressed. You don't have to be rich to feel scared and hoard or withhold. Greed is a symptom of fear, nothing more. It's not necessarily correlated with any financial status.

If you want to find examples of generosity, there are plenty out there! The National Philanthropic Trust reports that total American giving in 2005 was $260 billion and that giving has increased forty-one out of the last forty-two years. They also report that 89% of Americans give some money every year and 55% donate their time. If 89% of people are givers, look around and imagine that nine of ten people at the post office give and share.

Warren Buffet has a fortune estimated at $52 billion. In 2006, he announced that he was giving $30 billion worth of stock to the Bill and Melinda Gates foundation. "The Gates have set out to try to figure out how they can help the most human lives in the world," says Buffet. "It's not a bad deal."

The July 2007 issue of *Vanity Fair* magazine featured a variety of stories regarding Africa's health, money, politics and global sharing. One story was about Project (Red), a cooperative project between businesses and giving that involves corporations, consumers and possibility.

Individuals in First World countries buy cell phones and shoes and clothing designated (Red), and the companies from which they buy those products contribute a portion of their profits to distributing medicine to Africans in need. *Vanity Fair* reported that in the first nine months of the project, $25 million went from (Red) corporate partners to health care organizations fighting AIDS, tuberculosis and malaria. Project (Red) partners include American Express, Apple, Emporio Armani, Converse, Gap and Motorola. The participation of these large companies is a great example of a money game of co-creation.

The following is from the (Red) Manifesto: "(Red) is not a charity. It is simply a business model. You buy (Red) stuff, we get the money, buy the pills and distribute them. They take the pills, stay alive and continue to take care of their families and contribute socially and economically in their communities."

Another disempowering social idea is that rich people must have cheated, exploited or just inherited their money. *The Millionaire Next Door* by Thomas J. Stanley, PhD and William D. Danko, PhD is a great book because it readjusts our ideas about how wealth in America has been created. The millionaires the authors studied earned their financial status through savings, entrepreneurship and intention.

If you choose to believe that it is possible for rich people to create their riches through creativity, possibility and contribution, then you could do that as well. You could also extend a blessing and an encouragement to create more generosity, sharing and expansion for all.

The notion that the poor are needy and require pity and help is another disempowering idea for those who believe it and for those about whom they believe it. What if financial lack isn't really spiritual?

Spiritual teachers such as Jesus of Nazareth, Buddha and Mohammed were well-known for having a rich mentality because their physical and earthly needs were met anywhere they went. They were aware of the abundant and generous invisible nature of life and not attached or beholden to physical possessions. That's wealth consciousness, not poverty. They were so in service to the wholeness of the divine that they were able to manifest food, supply, miracles and healing from their activities. But being spiritual doesn't have to mean poor.

Mother Theresa was very humble and plainly-dressed, but she was infinitely powerful in the amount of money she raised to feed people and to serve others. By the late 1990's, she operated 517 missions in more than 100 countries. Over the years, Mother Teresa's Missionaries of Charity grew from twelve sisters to over 4,000, serving the poorest of the poor in 450 centers around the world.

What if the poor are not hopeless victims? If you view people who are struggling with survival as less than or beneath yourself and others, then you do not serve them. If you view everyone as having access to the infinite capacities of the divine, then you view people as always having the possibility for expressing themselves more, and you are of more help when you contribute to people in ways that build them up.

Helping People

How do healthy, wealthy, happy and prosperous people create a prosperous world? When you give from a sense that you're at one with a plentiful universe, what you give into and give from creates more of the same. Wayne Dyer says, "We cannot feel bad enough to make things better." This means that when other people are suffering, when there's a challenge in the world, or when there's a lack, feeling bad about it will not help.

The best thing you can do in any situation is to see everyone as whole and contribute a vibration of possibility. Then when you give money, time or service to provide for people's basic needs, you do so from respect.

In Abraham Maslow's *Hierarchy of Needs*, having basic physical safety and survival needs met is essential before people can build their capacity to work, to contribute and to be self-actualized. A Los Angeles spiritual center provides weekly meals to those who are hungry each Saturday morning at the Santa Monica City Hall. Everyone who participates, whether serving or eating or sharing, is responsible for setting up, serving, cleaning up and breaking down. That's the essence of sharing from wholeness.

Worrying about others, feeling sympathetic, and pitying others does not help them be empowered. Everyone has the capacity to contribute, no matter who they are. Pitying others separates. Seeing others whole unites.

There Is No "They"

In their financial lives, the usual targets people choose to demonize are entities and individuals such as the IRS, lawyers, their boss, the stock market, their ex or the government. While you may or may not agree with or like their behaviors, their choices or their particular values, it's important on a spiritual level to understand that everything is a creation of consciousness.

At some level, whether individually or collectively, you created the things you demonize. Therefore, the best thing you can do to enhance your relationship with those individuals and institutions is to shift into a point of view of integrity, clarity and generosity. I encourage you to think about any monetary transaction or relationship with the highest level of respect and integrity you can.

I have been to wealth-building seminars where there was an abundance of energy spent on not paying any more taxes than one is supposed to. How much time, energy and attention are spent in avoiding paying taxes? Of course, you should be smart and make the best financial choices for yourself, your family and the world. But don't be afraid. Don't be mad. If you want to change the government, get involved in politics. Living in anger and fear about a particular entity or group only creates more anger and fear. Spend your time and energy co-creating your wealth vision.

Win/Win

Warren Buffet is a big proponent of the win/win scenario. He doesn't negotiate a deal from the perspective of taking advantage of his competitor. He approaches the negotiation as the creation of a partnership in which both sides receive a fair exchange for value and are happy with the arrangement. This produces a very effective ongoing relationship and increases overall profitability.

This doesn't mean you get soft; it means you get creative and create a win-win negotiation. This is creatively breaking through into the particular needs and interests of each side so there is collaboration rather than compromise, taking the negotiation to a higher level.

Stewardship

Stewardship is about caring for what you have with consciousness, respect and dignity, therefore contributing to respect and appreciation all around. Stewardship of the Earth is being conscious of the flow of products and services you buy, use, recycle and discard. Stewardship is shopping, spending and circulating with suppliers, buyers and vendors whose ethics, practices and policies you want to support.

An Organizational View

Richard Whiteley is the founder of The Whiteley Group, a global firm dedicated to helping people and companies reach their potential. Richard is affectionately known by his clients and colleagues as the "corporate shaman" for his capacity to link deeply mystic native practices to the bottom-line realities of for-profit corporate life. Richard has presented to over 150,000 executives in twenty-six countries and authored several best-selling books, including *Love the Work You're With*. I asked Richard for his view about money and its meaning in corporate life.

"Money has many meanings organizationally. It's a very clear indicator of success in a for-profit operation. If you are a for-profit organization and you don't make a profit, then you are not successful. That is the long and the short of it.

A second meaning is that it's a way of sustaining your growth and sustaining the organization in the future. Are you successful or not? Can you sustain yourself into the future? How are you doing relative to others in your industry and in other industries?

I think the greatest trouble is letting money become too dominant in our lives. As an organization, having a kind of manic drive toward the bottom-line can zap the spirit right out of a company. It becomes hollow. I have seen this happen over and over again. People are not inspired to work for money. They are inspired to work for a cause. People work in reverse order: They will work harder for a good leader than they will for money, and they will work harder for a cause than for a good leader.

In companies like Tom's of Maine, you find organizations with a very clear statement of values. They link values to people to profits. They live by the values that they espouse. People want work that has meaning, and meaning comes from a value-driven organization. The money-making has value that people can feel and relate to.

The world is waking up in the field of leadership around connections, communication and meaning. The hardest person to lead is yourself, and I think we are going to see much more personal growth and direct attention put on self-leadership. I'm inspired by what I see emerging in new leaders coming into the workplace. We are meaning-makers in whatever enterprise we're engaged in."

Your Legacy, Our Legacy

What is your wealth legacy, including spirituality, beliefs and habits? What money map are you going to leave to the next generation? The number one thing you leave to your family, children, parents, siblings, community, and spiritual family is the model of how you lived. The universal reality you serve, what you believe, how you act, what you say, and what you have done is the greatest legacy you can leave behind.

Remember also that the quality of the legacy you leave is as important as the quantity. If you're not already there, get yourself organized when it comes to trusts, wills and a healthcare power of attorney. You want your choices and your habits to line up with what you believe.

What's the legacy you're leaving? If you were to die today, what would you leave behind? Think about the invisible, spiritual qualities, your beliefs and the values you've been living. Think about the visible results you leave behind.

Numerous financial planning programs and models are based on the assumption that the future will be an exact replica of the past. It's one way you can measure the compound value of savings. But spiritually, we have no way of predicting the certainty of the future in an ever-changing universe.

I'm not saying don't save money. Just remember that life is about transformation and growth. Take care of your inner world, and your outer world will flow with what needs to flow.

Then what's the best way to plan for the future? The only plan for the future that can lead to peace of mind is to stay in the flow of spiritual truth here in the present moment. Continue to expand your realization of your magnificent spiritual reality. And continue to set goals for both quality and results. But know that conditions, circumstances and things of this world change. Your peace doesn't come from them. The political systems, the economic systems, the technological systems, the currency systems, the health systems and the communication systems are going to change.

When you stop worrying, resenting or frantically manipulating things, people and events in your personal money life, you have so much more capacity to be of genuine and profound service to the world. You give your time, energy and attention to projects, people and possibility. The Money Keys website will always have a link to the "A Wealthy World" List of Love, the latest in inspiring projects, people and groups you can support.

Conclusion

The secret to walking through the doorway into your vision of real financial power is that you are already created in the image and likeness of an eternal, immortal, infinite, abundant and loving divine presence. When you cultivate your realization of this spiritual truth, you are at peace, you are free and you are powerful. That's it. You're done!

You're already as spiritual as you are ever going to be. So, spiritual growth really is a paradox. The nature of the divine, although complete, is to ever expand. There's always more of the infinite to express. You are both complete and ever-expanding.

Continue to grow at your perfect pace. You live, grow and express best in cycles of action and reflection, stillness and movement. That's how you learn. That's how life happens. And everybody has his or her own pace and rhythm. Find yours.

Money isn't everything. It isn't anything, really, except for the meaning you give it. I trust you are more capable now to vision, manage, flow and share your money in a way that reveals more of you and serves the world.

I'm grateful that you have invested your time, energy and resources here. I know that you are moving forward into your life with power and with possibility. I love you, I bless you, and I wish you well.

Chapter Nine Review

Questions for Reflection

1) What do rich and poor mean to me? Are there any beliefs about myself or others that I need to dissolve?

2) Are there any individuals or groups I make into a "they" around money? What if there is no "they?"

3) How do I relate to the spiritual paradox that I am both "whole and complete" and "ever-expanding?" What does it have to do with my individual wealth and my relationship to the world?

Ideas for Action

1) Create and share a Living Legacy.

- Be sure the people you care about know what reality you serve, what game you play, and what growth you're committed to around money and its meaning in your life.

- Write or record your money eulogy and articulate the legacy of your consciousness, your vision and your values.

- Share your money eulogy through a live conversation or through a family meeting by creating a CD or video or storybook.

Tools

Visit **www.themoneykeys.com/tools** to download the *"Wealthy World" List of Love*, projects, people and groups committed to building a wealthy world for all. Find connections to places where you can share your time, talent and resources.

About the Author

Karen Russo is the author of *The Money Keys: Unlocking Peace, Freedom and Real Financial Power.* Karen is your angel of affluence in conscious wealth building, your spiritual advisor in personal finance, and your guide in taking your money life from mundane to masterful.

Karen delivers keynote speeches and facilitates seminars all over the world, connecting with audiences of many different backgrounds, including investors, entrepreneurs, business professionals, and spiritual seekerss. With her trademark blend of spiritual clarity and real world humor, her style is both down-to-earth and out of this world.

Karen shares her expertise from both the secular and spiritual realms. With an MBA from Columbia University, Karen has devoted 20 years to the corporate world of finance, marketing and consulting. She also studied for over a decade with Michael Bernard Beckwith, Founder of the Agape Spiritual Center. She recently became an ordained minister-for-life with the United Centers of Spiritual Living. A late-in-life first time newlywed, Karen lives in Arizona with her beloved Bill. She is also the creator of inspirational programs for women, *Your Beautiful Spirit.*

To schedule keynote presentations, seminars or retreats with Karen Russo, please call 877. 249. 0194, email customercare@ themoneykeys.com, or go to www.themoneykeys.com.

The Money Keys Resources

We are committed to helping you prosper in every way.

Visit www.themoneykeys.com for the following:

- Books, music and articles for your ongoing education and inspiration
- Teleseminars on Spiritual Laws and Spiritual Practices for Peace, Freedom and Possibility
- Karen Russo's speaking and workshop schedule
- Links to counselors, services, educational programs, products, businesses, charities and people we love and recommend

If you have questions, suggestions or successes you would like to share, we want to hear from you!

Please contact us at:

Live Your Truth Enterprises, LLC
6929 N. Hayden Rd, #C4-476
Scottsdale AZ 85252-7970
877-249-0194
customercare@themoneykeys.com
www.themoneykeys.com/tools

Are you Ready to Put *The Money Keys* into Action?

Enjoy an even deeper experience of the spiritual principles and practical tools of Karen Russo's *The Money Keys*.

- Stay inspired, empowered and successful in your money life.
- Enjoy Karen's expert teaching on applying the Laws of Unity, Creation & Circulation with step-by-step instruction and examples
- Strengthen your regular spiritual practices with guided visioning, meditations and exercises

The Money Keys Audio CD Library includes 5 volumes:

- 20 CD's with 120+ pages of exercises, worksheets and application tools
- Escaping the Money Traps
- Spirituality: Finding Permanent Peace of Mind
- Beliefs: Choosing Freedom
- Habits: Get into the Flow
- Your People, Your Partner, Your World

(Volumes sold separately)

Bonus! The program includes:
- Powerful music tracks from contemporary artists
- PDF files of worksheets & tools
- Links to online tools
- Membership to monthly ezine with tips, stories and new teaching
- A one-on-one session with a spiritual coach
- Access to group coaching tele-calls with Karen Russo

Musician
Orgena Rose

Visit www.themoneykeys.com or call 877 249 0194 to sample audio tracks and learn more. Use coupon code **bookreader** at checkout for special savings.

877-249-0194 | www.themoneykeys.com | info@revkarenrusso.com

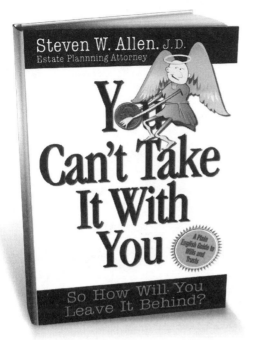

Build Mastery with the Law Of Attraction:
The Quintessential Guide To Conscious Creation

Through the **Law of Attraction**, you were born with unlimited power to create your life exactly how you want it.

- **How much are your beliefs really costing you?**
- Start out on a lifetime of attracting what you want
- **Awaken your incredible power lying hidden inside**
- Discover the four simple steps of Conscious Creation
- **Experience genuine, lasting inner peace and joy**
- Raise your vibrations & become a magnet for your desires

Visit www.UniverseOfPower.com/courses to learn more.

Give Out Loud™

Our Vision :

To offer a platform for people around the globe to inspire and participate in a community for giving.

To raise the level of consciousness of the world so that compassion is the fuel that eliminates hunger & poverty and, education and mentorship shifts community thinking from that of hopelessness to that of hope and inspiration.

It all starts with you....Join us today and be part of history.

www.giveoutloud.com

OTHER BOOKS FROM LifeSuccess Publishing

You Were Born Rich

Bob Proctor
ISBN # 978-0-9656264-1-5

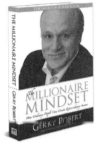

The Millionaire Mindset
*How Ordinary People Can
Create Extraordinary Income*

Gerry Robert
ISBN # 978-1-59930-030-6

Rekindle The Magic In
Your Relationship
Making Love Work

Anita Jackson
ISBN # 978-1-59930-041-2

Finding The Bloom of
The Cactus Generation
*Improving the quality of
life for Seniors*

Maggie Walters
ISBN # 978-1-59930-011-5

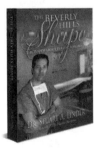

The Beverly Hills Shape
The Truth About Plastic Surgery

Dr. Stuart Linder
ISBN # 978-1-59930-049-8

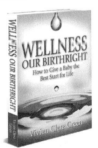

Wellness Our Birthright
*How to give a baby the best
start in life.*

Vivien Clere Green
ISBN # 978-1-59930-020-7

Lighten Your Load

Peter Field
ISBN # 978-1-59930-000-9

Change & How To
Survive In The New
Economy
*7 steps to finding freedom
& escaping the rat race*

Barrie Day
ISBN # 978-1-59930-015-3

OTHER BOOKS FROM LIFESUCCESS PUBLISHING

Stop Singing The Blues
*10 Powerful Strategies For
Hitting The High Notes In
Your Life*

Dr. Cynthia Barnett
ISBN # 978-1-59930-022-1

Don't Be A Victim,
*Protect Yourself
Everything Seniors Need To
Know To Avoid Being Taken
Financially*

Jean Ann Dorrell
ISBN # 978-1-59930-024-5

A "Hand Up", not a
"Hand Out"
*The best ways to help others
help themselves*

David Butler
ISBN # 978-1-59930-071-9

Doctor Your Medicine Is
Killing Me!
*One Mans Journey From
Near Death to Health and
Wellness*

Pete Coussa
ISBN # 978-1-59930-047-4

I Believe in Me
*7 Ways for Woman to Step
Ahead in Confidence*

Lisa Gorman
ISBN # 978-1-59930-069-6

The Color of Success
*Why Color Matters in your
Life, your Love, your Lexus*

Mary Ellen Lapp
ISBN # 978-1-59930-078-8

If Not Now, When?
What's Your Dream?

Cindy Nielsen
ISBN # 978-1-59930-073-3

The Skills to Pay the
Bills... and then some!
*How to inspire everyone in
your organisation into high
performance!*

Buki Mosaku
ISBN # 978-1-59930-058-0